# SCOOUWA: James Smith's Indian Captivity Narrative

William M. Darlington's
illustrative notes from the 1870
Clarke edition are included
with additional annotation
by John J. Barsotti, Assistant Curator,
Ohio Historical Society.

Ohio Historical Society
Thomas H. Smith, Ph.D., Director
Columbus, Ohio
1978

2

Originally published under the title, An Account of the Remarkable Occurrences in the Life and Travels of Col. James Smith, . . . by John Bradford of Lexington in 1799.

ISBN 0-87758-009-X
LC 77-90430

Printed in the United States of America.

# Contents

# Illustrations and Maps

# Foreword

As James Smith reflected, "occurrences truly and plainly stated as they happened . . . make the best history." Smith's sensitive yet unemotional captivity journal illustrates man's basic struggle for survival in an unbroken wilderness: the precarious lives of the Indians, the European influences on their customs and dress, and later the continuing battles between settlers, loyalists, and traders. As Smith's journal evolves, his captors become more than brutal tomahawk-swinging scalp collectors for he reveals the varied dimensions of Indian customs and culture. Too frequently these aspects of Indian life are forgotten in novelized visions of a bloody, impassioned frontier. Therefore, the Ohio Historical Society is reprinting the journal Colonel Smith wrote during his captivity to make the "best history" readily available again to both the historian and the casual reader.

This is the eighth edition of Colonel James Smith's complete journal. Originally printed in 1799 by John Bradford in Lexington, Kentucky, an abridged 1812 edition, "A Treatise on the Mode and Manner of Indian Wars," was printed in Paris, Kentucky, by Joel R. Lyle. J. Grigg of Philadelphia printed the third edition in 1831. Three years later Grigg and Elliot of Philadelphia printed the next edition and in 1838 the fifth edition was printed in Philadelphia. Robert Clarke & Company of Cincinnati printed an annotated sixth edition in 1870 and later the seventh edition in 1907. As one of the best Indian captivity narratives, this journal has been reprinted in whole or in part in various captivity collections during the last one hundred and fifty years. It was also the basis for at least one fictional account of the life and times of Colonel James Smith.

Throughout this volume, William M. Darlington's annotations from the 1870 edition have been italicized; in a few instances Darlington's annotations have been abridged. In keeping with Smith's statement that "nature always outshines art," his original 1799 punctuation, capitalization, and spelling have been retained.

We thank Charles Pittenger, museum curator of the Kentucky Historical Society, who helped us find the current owner of the Smith portrait, Warren J. Shonert of Falmouth, Kentucky.

In addition to annotator John J. Barsotti, Ohio Historical Society staff members who assisted in the preparation of this publication are: William Keener, Chief of the Education Division; Thomas H. Hartig, Chief of the History Department; James K. Richards, Chief of the Publications Division; typist Cynthia L. Reed; editor Clare Wulker, and illustrator Bruce R. Baby who did the interior graphics and cover design.

The Ohio Historical Society
1978

# Biography*

James Smith was born in 1737, in Franklin county, Pennsylvania, at that time the backwoods frontier, the extreme limit of civilization. As might be expected, he received but a limited education in book-learning, but, as befitted a backwoods boy, he was well versed in wood-craft, active in the hunt, and inured to all the hardships and trials of a frontier life. At the age of eighteen, in 1755, he was taken captive by the Indians, was adopted into one of their families, and accompanied them in all their wanderings, till his escape in 1759. He returned to Conococheague early in 1760, and was received with great joy by his family and friends.

He settled himself at his old home in the ordinary routine of pioneer farming, and in May, 1763, married Miss Anne Wilson, by whom he had seven children—four sons, Jonathan, William, James, and Robert; and three daughters, Jane, Elizabeth, and Rebecca. His subsequent adventures, as a leader of the Black-boys, in 1763 and 1769; his service as a lieutenant in Bouquet's expedition against the Ohio Indians in 1764; his exploring excursion into southern Kentucky in 1766, and his services during the Revolutionary war, in which he earned and received the rank of colonel, are sufficiently detailed in his own narrative.

After the temporary peace made with the Indians in 1778, he removed to Westmoreland county, Pennsylvania, and settled on a farm on Jacob's creek. Here his wife died. Of her we know little, except that she was a good woman, and a devoted wife and mother. In 1785, he spent most of the summer in Kentucky, looking after some land claims; there he married his second wife, Mrs. Margaret Irvin, nee Rodgers, widow of Mr. Abraham Irvin, a woman of cultivated mind, with whom he lived happily until her decease in 1800. They had no children. She had five by her former marriage.

*Reprinted from the 1870 Clarke edition.

Of Mr. Smith's affection for his first wife, the following incident bears witness. It was communicated to us by Rev. J. M. Smith, son of Mr. Smith's youngest son, Robert.

"My father's earliest recollections related to the habits of his father, which he told about as follows: His mother was buried on the farm, on a hill at some distance from the house, where some large oak trees had been left standing to mark and shade the family burying ground. Under the shade of these trees my grandfather had constructed a kind of booth, somewhat after the form of an Indian wigwam, but small in size. In this he had made a couch, upon which he would lie upon his back and read. To this retreat he was accustomed to take his little son, and there to read to him from the Holy Scriptures, and point out to him the grave of his mother. Their last visit to this hallowed spot made a very deep impression upon the mind of my father; he never referred to it without tears, even when he was an old man. They were about to remove to the State of Kentucky, and all other matters having been arranged, he took his little boy and repaired to the grave of his wife, which he was soon to leave forever, and there the two kneeled, side by side, and the widowed husband offered up his last prayer on behalf of his orphan child over the grave of the departed wife and mother. This done, leading his little son by the hand, he followed his family, who had already started from their old home to seek a new one in the wilds of Kentucky."

This was in 1788. He took with him, his wife and her children, and of his own children, James, William, Robert, and Rebecca, and settled on Cane Ridge, in Bourbon county, Kentucky, about seven miles from Paris.

Col. Smith was a man of very quiet and taciturn character, a reader and a thinker, and much given to religious reading and meditation. In him, however, the courage of opinion was fully developed, and when roused, he had more than ordinary talent in debate, so that among his new neighbors he soon became a man of mark. He was elected the same year a member of the convention which sat at Danville to confer about a separation from the State of Virginia, and afterward represented Bourbon county in the General Assembly of the State.

In religious matters Col. Smith was an enthusiast, and for some time took an active part in the Stoneite movement, which so excited the early church in Kentucky, for an account of which we must refer our readers to Davidson's History of the Presbyterian Church in Kentucky. He finally, however, returned to the Presbyterian church, and receiving licensure, or perhaps ordination, he spent much of his time in his later years as a missionary among the Indians, for which work his familiarity with Indian character eminently fitted him.

In 1802 he lived with his son James, to whom he had conveyed the copyright and the remaining copies of his work, and also twenty acres of land, for which the son had agreed "to decently support his father during his lifetime."

On his return from one of his missionary excursions into Tennessee, he found that his son James had during his absence joined the Shakers, and had gone with his family to a settlement which that sect had just formed on Turtle Creek, Ohio (near Lebanon). He followed, "to see what sort of people they were," lived with them only a short time, but long enough to be disgusted with the whole fraternity. His son James, who before joining the Shakers "was naturally friendly, a dutiful son, a kind husband and a tender father," seems to have changed his whole nature, and "appeared to be divested of natural affection toward his wife Polly and other connections." She, on going to visit some relatives with her father-in-law, was advertised by her husband as having left his "house and board without any just cause;" and on her return, at the instigation of the elders, he refused to receive her, or allow her to see her children, "without she would receive their testimony." Thus driven from the settlement, and from her husband and children, she returned to her friends in Kentucky. Col. Smith was greatly exasperated at the conduct of his son, and opened his batteries on the leaders of the Shakers, exposing them socially, theologically, and politically, in a pamphlet entitled

"REMARKABLE OCCURRENCES lately discovered among the People called SHAKERS: of a Treasonable and barbarous nature; or, SHAKERISM DEVELOPED. By James Smith. Paris (Ky.) Printed by Joel R. Lyle." (1810.) pp. 24.

This brought out a rejoinder by Richard McNemar, one of their leaders, and Col. Smith again appeared in print, in a pamphlet of 44 pages, entitled

"SHAKERISM DETECTED; their Erroneous and Treasonable Proceedings, and FALSE PUBLICATIONS contained in Different Newspapers, Exposed to Public View, by the depositions of ten different persons living in various parts of the State of Kentucky and Ohio, accompanied with remarks. By Col. James Smith, of Kentucky. Paris, Kentucky. Printed by Joel R. Lyle. 1810."

These, however, had no result so far as the son was concerned: he remained with the Shakers; and Col. Smith spent the remainder of his days, thus embittered by the unnatural conduct of his son, chiefly with his step-children, the Irvins, in Washington county, Kentucky, where he died in 1812.

The Indians had again become very troublesome in 1811, and a general Indian war was expected. Col. Smith, now too old for actual service,* but still having considerable of the old leaven of patriotism in him, wrote out and published a treatise on Indian warfare, of which the following is the title page:

"A Treatise on the Mode and Manner of Indian War, their Tactics, Discipline and Encampment, the various Methods they Practise, in order to obtain the Advantage, by Ambush, Surprise, Surrounding, &c. Ways and Means proposed to Prevent the Indians from obtaining the Advantage. A Chart, or Plan of Marching, and Encamping, laid down, whereby we may undoubtedly Surround them, if we have Men Sufficient. Also—A Brief Account of Twenty-three Campaigns, carried on against the Indians with the Events since the year 1755; Gov. Harrison's included. By Col. James Smith. Likewise—Some Abstracts selected from his Journal, while in Captivity with the Indians, relative to the Wars: which was published many years ago, but few of them now to be found. Paris Kentucky. Printed by Joel R. Lyle. 1812." pp I, 59.

There is not much new matter in this volume. It is little more than those portions of his "captivity" relating to Indian warfare, rearranged and connected. No one could read it without being convinced of the wisdom of the tactics he suggests and even of their applicability to Indian warfare in these latter days.

We must express our obligations to Miss Sarah M'Quaid, of Elizabeth, Pennsylvania, who was brought up in Jonathan Smith's family, and Rev. J. M. Smith, of McKeesport, Pennsylvania, for much of the material of this sketch; and also to Rev. Joel K. Lyle, of Lexington, for the use of the two Shaker pamphlets; and Mr. S. B. Elliott, of Cincinnati, for the pamphlet on Indian warfare.

* He made the attempt, however. In Niles' Register for September 26, 1812, he is said to have "gone to join the army, when he heard of the surrender of Hull." His son Robert raised a company of volunteers in Washington county, Ky. He was a tanner, and in order to uniform his company he tanned all their pantaloons in his vats.

# Introduction

After the Revolutionary War, when French and British claims to the Ohio country had been extinguished, an aging Indian reflected on his people's role in their struggle for this area. Comparing England and France to the blades of a scissors, he concluded, "we are the cloth." European penetration had been marked by tri-partite maneuvering, with both "civilized" nations seeking to enlist the tribes as military allies and commercial patrons. The Indian response was a shifting pattern of loyalties and allegiances, based on the hope that the imperial conflict could be used to their own advantage, which was variously bolstered or undermined by a structure of ancient inter-tribal feuds and friendships. Unremitting, amidst the vagaries of the contest, was the constant rending of the cloth until its integrity was destroyed.

By the early 1700s, the inter-tribal warfare which had made Ohio uninhabitable in the seventeenth century had subsided. Many tribes moved freely in the area between the Great Lakes and the Ohio River, and several major groups—Ottawa, Delaware, Wyandot, Shawnee, Miami, and Mingo—established themselves as permanent residents.

An extensive intermingling was common among the Ohio tribes. Iroquoian long houses and Algonquian wigwams stood side by side in many villages. Several tribal affiliations were commonly represented in any war party. In council and the chase—even in choosing a spouse —tribal barriers were easily crossed. Shared in common was a life-style increasingly dependent on trade with one or the other of the European powers and the nagging consciousness that the Indian was at an increasing disadvantage because of that dependence. The desire to reach an accommodation with the white man which would secure a share of his material wealth was offset by a growing body of experience which demonstrated the destructiveness of such accommodation. All the tribes watched uneasily the imperial struggle, hesitating to choose sides, yet fearing that neutrality would diminish their influence. Smith recounts the Wyandot myth that the land had been bequeathed to them by a revered "great-grandmother," a belief that had its counterpart in every tribal tradition. All were aggrieved at the prospect of its loss through failures of war or diplomacy over which they had little control.

British imperialism crossed the Alleghenies in the packs of Pennsylvania and Virginia fur traders. The clientage of the Six Nations, who were the nominal overlords of the Ohio Valley tribes, seemed to Englishmen a sufficient counter to the claims of France. George Croghan and Conrad Weiser, agents of the Pennsylvania legislature, feverishly proselytized among the Ohio Indians in the 1740s. The notable expedition of Celoron de Blainville in 1749 was designed to assert a French title based on the right of discovery and the provisions of several treaties, principally that of Utrecht in 1713. His report to Montreal affirmed the presence of numerous British traders and their considerable influence among the Ohio tribes. Threatening and cajoling, he had made his way among the Indian towns. He found no promise in the sullen and equivocal responses of the natives that their patronage of the English would be abandoned. French anxiety was compounded by a parliamentary grant of 500,000 acres bordering the Ohio River to a combination of enterprising Virginians. In 1750 as the agent of this Ohio Company, Christopher Gist traveled as far as the present site of Louisville. He was cordially received at Pickawillany, the Miami capital, where Celoron's blandishments had gone unheeded the previous year.

Months of desultory raiding ensued, including the destruction of Pickawillany by French-led Ottawas in 1752. As the struggle intensified, the "Forks of the Ohio" drew the attention of strategists on both sides. This juncture, where the Allegheny and Monongahela rivers came together to form the Ohio, was the military key to the entire Ohio River watershed. In 1754 Virginia's Governor Dinwiddie ordered the building of a fort at the forks. Before the works could be completed, a French force, supported by a chain of outposts anchored at Presque Isle, routed the Virginians. Militia under George Washington arrived too late to prevent the French success, was itself invested in hastily-built Fort Necessity, and capitulated. French arms held sway on the upper Ohio, based on the appropriated works at the forks, now christened Fort Duquesne.

In London, Parliament took up the gage, dispatching Major General Edward Braddock and 1,400 regulars who landed in Virginia in April of 1755. The long-roll had sounded in what Winston Churchill would denominate the "First World War," a war which would magnify British influence around the globe, but nowhere so much as on the North

American continent. Reinforced by colonial militiamen, General Braddock moved in the early summer of 1755 to dislodge the French from
the Forks of the Ohio. Near the line of Braddock's advance, a party of
Pennsylvanians was engaged in road building. The young James Smith
was among them. His story begins with this letter from Colonel James
Burd, a road commissioner, to Pennsylvania's Governor Morris:

"FROM THE ALLEGHENY MOUNTAINS,
"5th July, 1755.

"HONORED SIR: We have now got this far with the road, but at present
are under a very great dilemma, the cause of which is as follows: We had
thought it necessary to make use of an empty house, 47 miles from
Anthony Thompson's, for a store-house for our provisions, and we sent
a guard of seven men, armed, to said store-house. They immediately
fortified the house, and had received some of our provisions. We were
like to be short of meat, etc., and hearing that there were wagons, and
supposing cattle, upon the road, one Mr. Robert McCay, who had the
command of the store and the people there, sent a boy called James
Smith, about sixteen years of age, down the road to hurry up the cattle
and wagons. Said Smith meeting a man sent up by Mr. Adam Hoops, at
Ray's Town, received information that the wagons were just at hand,
upon which the boy returned with Mr. Hoops' man hither, the wagons
at this time being behind. The wagons arrived at the store the 3d
curr't, at noon. Inquiry was made of the wagoners where Mr. Hoops'
man and the boy were, and they replied that they had not seen them;
upon which they went out to search for them. They first found the boy's
hat, and then Mr. Hoops' man's (named Arnold Vigorous) gun, and
about ten perches from thence, Arnold lying dead, being shot through
with two bullets and scalped. Mr. McCay immediately dispatched an
express to me to the camp, about twelve miles from the store. I went
down with a party of twelve men of Captain Hogg's company, and saw
the corpse and got it buried, but can find nothing of the boy, only his
horse we have got. That night, being the evening of the 3d curr't, we
mounted guard at the store. About 9 o'clock we were attacked by
Indians; their number we could not know. Two of our sentinels fired
at two of the Indians which they saw, and I myself pursued singly the
said two Indians, but being dark amongst the trees, could not see them
nor overtake them, but heard them plainly about fifteen yards before
me. The next day, being the 4th curr't, I returned to our camp, and was
under a necessity to call the people together, and made use of all the

arguments I could to induce them to continue in the service until we had finished. But, unfortunately, we had an alarm last night. One of the sentinels on the picket guard challenged three times and fired his musket, which has struck a great terror into the laborers; thirty of them are gone home this morning, and the remainder are very much dissatisfied, as they have no arms, and I am really afraid we shall not be able to keep them much longer. However, the Governor may depend upon my utmost endeavors to carry on the work, and that I won't leave my duty while I have ten men to work, or am recalled by your Honor.

"We are obliged to send off this morning a guard of twelve men and a sergeant of Captain Hogg's Company for a covering party for our returning wagons, and to bring up our provisions from the inhabitants, as we can't so much as hunt up our horses but with a guard. Our roads are all waylaid in order to cut off our provisions and any straggling men they can. Mr. William Smith is likewise under a necessity to go home this morning, as the boy that is taken prisoner (as we suppose) is his brother-in-law. We have now about three days' provisions.

"Please to excuse unconnections.

"I am, respectfully, your Honor's most obed't, h'ble, servant,

"JAMES BURD."

"TO THE HONORABLE GOVERNOR MORRIS."

On facing page: Original Title Page

# AN ACCOUNT

## OF THE

# REMARKABLE OCCURRENCES

### IN THE LIFE AND TRAVELS OF

# Col. JAMES SMITH,

*(Now a Citizen of Bourbon County, Kentucky,)*

**DURING HIS CAPTIVITY WITH THE INDIANS,**

**IN THE YEARS 1755, '56, '57, '58, & '59,**

In which the Cuſtoms, Manners, Traditions, Theological Sentiments, Mode of Warfare, Military Tactics, Diſcipline and
Encampments, Treatment of priſoners, &c. are better ex-
plained, and more minutely related, than has been heretofore
done, by any author on that ſubject. Together with a De-
ſcription of the Soil, Timber and Waters, where he travelled with the Indians, during his captivity.

**TO WHICH IS ADDED,**

A Brief Account of ſome Very Uncommon Occurrences, which
tranſpired after his return from captivity; as well as of the
Different Campaigns carried on againſt the Indians to the
weſtward of Fort Pitt, ſince the year 1755, to the preſent
date.

## WRITTEN BY HIMSELF.

*LEXINGTON:*
PRINTED BY JOHN BRADFORD, ON MAIN STREET,

1799.

# PREFACE

I was strongly urged to publish the following work, immediately after my return from captivity, which was nearly forty years ago — but, as at that time the Americans were so little acquainted with Indian affairs, I apprehended a great part of it would be viewed as fable or romance.

As the Indians never attempted to prevent me either from reading or writing, I kept a Journal, which I revised shortly after my return from captivity, and which I have kept ever since: and as I have had but a moderate English education, have been advised to employ some person of liberal education to transcribe and embellish it — but believing that nature always outshines art, have thought, that occurrences truly and plainly stated, as they happened, would make the best history, be better understood, and most entertaining.

In the different Indian speeches copied into this work, I have not only imitated their own style, or mode of speaking, but have also preserved the

Nature always outshines art—In keeping with this belief, Smith's original spelling, punctuation, capitalization, and mode of expression have been retained.

When defence is necessary — Smith published his narrative four years after the signing of the Greene Ville Treaty which was to bring peace to the Ohio Valley. At this time the brilliant Shawnee leader, Tecumseh, was just beginning to develop his plan for a grand Indian confederacy to resist the flood of settlers threatening to displace the Indians east of the Mississippi. No leader since Pontiac in 1763 had succeeded in uniting the various Indian tribes, but now it seemed that Tecumseh might. Having fought in Pontiac's War, Colonel Smith easily could have compared Tecumseh's growing reputation for leadership with Pontiac's. Smith may have wanted to warn the people of 1799 that another struggle with the Indians might be coming up.

ideas meant to be communicated in those speeches — In common conversation, I have used my own style, but preserved their ideas. The principal advantage that I expect will result to the public, from the publication of the following sheets, is the observations on the Indian mode of warfare. Experience has taught the Americans the necessity of adopting their mode, and the more perfect we are in that mode, the better we shall be able to defend ourselves against them, when defence is necessary.

JAMES SMITH.

Bourbon County, June 1st, 1799.

# REMARKABLE OCCURRENCES, &c.

In May 1755, the province of Pennsylvania, agreed to send out three hundred men, in order to cut a waggon road from Fort Loudon, to join Braddock's road, near the Turkey Foot, or three forks of Yohogania. My brother-in-law, William Smith esq. of Conococheague, was appointed commissioner, to have the oversight of these road-cutters.

Though I was at that time only eighteen years of age, I had fallen violently in love with a young lady, whom I apprehended was possessed of a large share of both beauty and virtue; — but being born between Venus and Mars, I concluded I must also leave my dear fair one, and go out with this company of road-cutters, to see the event of this campaign; but still expecting that some time in the course of this summer, I should again return to the arms of my beloved.

We went on with the road, without interruption, until near the Allegheny Mountain; when I was sent back, in order to hurry up some provisions waggons that were on the way after us; I proceeded down the road as far as the crossings of Juniata, where, finding the waggons were coming on as fast as possible, I returned up the road again towards the

* Darlington

*Fort Loudon — Fort Loudon was erected in the year 1756, near the site of the present town of Loudon, in Franklin county, Pennsylvania. It was named in honor of John Campbell, Earl of Loudon, appointed on March 20, 1756, Commander-in-chief of all the forces in North America.

Conocheague—This town is now Mercersburg in Franklin County, Pennsylvania.

Early Provincial Roads— In 1750 an Ohio Company agent, Col. Thomas Cresap, sought to blaze a trail over the Laurel Hills to the Monongahela. His Indian guide, Nemacolin, pointed out an old Indian trace which had apparently been an over-mountain buffalo trail. After widening it, Cresap named it Nemacolin's Path. George Washington followed this path in 1753 when he threatened the French at Fort LeBoeuf and in 1754 when he was defeated at Fort Necessity. Braddock followed this road to disaster the next year.

Braddock's road was opened in May and June, 1755, from Fort Cumberland to the Great Crossings of the Youghiogheny (now Smithfield), by nearly the same line as that of the present

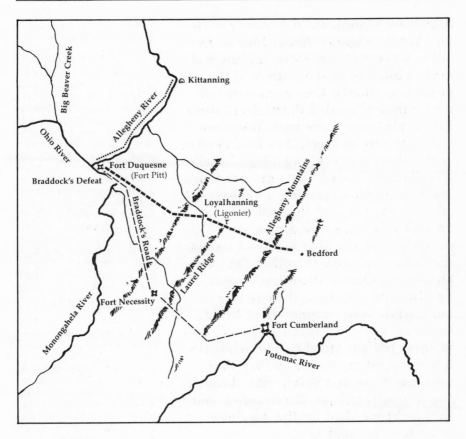

## Map 1

| | |
|---|---|
| ----- | Summer, 1755: Bedford area to Fort Duquesne. |
| ......... | Summer, 1755: Fort Duquesne to Kittanning. |

Allegheny Mountain, in company with one Arnold Vigoras. About four or five miles above Bedford, three Indians had made a blind of bushes, stuck in the ground, as though they grew naturally, where they concealed themselves, about fifteen yards from the road. When we came opposite to them, they fired upon us, at this short distance, and killed my fellow traveller, yet their bullets did not touch me; but my horse making a violent start, threw me, and the Indians immediately ran up, and took me prisoner. The one that laid hold on me was a Canasatauga, the other two were Delawares. One of them could speak English, and asked me if there were any more white men coming after? I told them not any near, that I knew of. Two of these Indians stood by me, whilst the other scalped my comrade: they then set off and ran at a smart rate, through the woods, for about fifteen miles, and that night we slept on the Alegheny Mountain, without fire.

The next morning they divided the last of their provision which they had brought from Fort DuQuesne, and gave me an equal share, which was about two or three ounces of mouldy biscuit—this and a young Ground-Hog, about as large as a Rabbit, roasted, and also equally divided, was all the provision we had until we came to the Loyal-Hannan, which was about fifty miles; and a great part of the way we came through exceeding rocky Laurel-thickets, without any path. When we came to the West side of Laurel-Hill, they gave the scalp

National road. Smithfield is about four miles from the Turkeyfoot.

General Braddock and the Quartermaster General, Sir John St. Clair, urgently solicited Governor Morris and the Council of Pennsylvania to order the construction of a road from the inhabited parts of the province westward toward the Ohio, to facilitate supplies of troops and provisions, as there was no wagon road through the mountains west of Carlisle, "only a horse-path used by the Indian traders." Accordingly, the Governor and Council directed a road to be made from Shippensburgh to the Youghiogheny. James Burd, Adam Hoops, George Croghan, William Smith (mentioned as "one of ye Commissioners of ye County" Cumberland), and others, were appointed Commissioners. They laid out the road; but, owing to the defeat of Braddock on the 9th of July, work on it was suspended; nor was it completed until a few years after the capture of Fort Du Quesne, in November, 1758. It traversed the present counties of Somerset, Bedford, Fulton, and part of Franklin. For many years it was known by the name of "Smith's road," from the circumstance of his capture on it during its construction, as related in his narrative.

Later it became the Cumberland Road. Differing only slightly in route, the National Road also followed Nemacolin's Path.

Ligoneer — *The town of Ligonier, in Westmoreland county, on the Loyalhanna creek and Philadelphia turnpike road, fifty miles east of Pittsburg. Fort Ligonier was erected here in 1758.*
The name of the Indian village was Loyalhanning or Middle Creek.

Fort Pitt — An English fort built in the Pittsburgh area in 1758.

halloo, as usual, which is a long yell or halloo, for every scalp or prisoner they have in possession; the last of these scalp halloos were followed with quick and sudden shrill shouts of joy and triumph. On their performing this, we were answered by the firing of a number of guns on the Loyal-Hannan, one after another, quicker than one could count, by another party of Indians, who were encamped near where Ligoneer now stands. As we advanced near this party, they increased with repeated shouts of joy and triumph; but I did not share with them in their excessive mirth. When we came to this camp, we found they had plenty of Turkeys and other meat, there; and though I never before eat venison without bread or salt, yet as I was hungry, it relished very well. There we lay that night, and the next morning the whole of us marched on our way for Fort DuQuesne. The night after we joined another camp of Indians, with nearly the same ceremony, attended with great noise, and apparent joy, among all, except one. The next morning we continued our march, and in the afternoon we came in full view of the fort, which stood on the point, near where Fort Pitt now stands. We then made a halt on the bank of the Alegheny, and repeated the scalp halloo, which was answered by the firing of all the firelocks in the hands of both Indians and French who were in and about the fort, in the aforesaid manner, and also the great guns, which were followed by the continued shouts and yells of the

different savage tribes who were then
collected there.

As I was at this time unacquainted
with this mode of firing and yelling of
the savages, I concluded that there were
thousands of Indians there, ready to
receive General Braddock; but what
added to my surprize, I saw numbers
running towards me, stripped naked,
excepting breech-clouts, and painted in
the most hideous manner, of various
colours, though the principal color was
vermillion, or a bright red; yet there was
annexed to this, black, brown, blue, &c.
As they approached, they formed
themselves into two long ranks, about
two or three rods apart. I was told by an
Indian that could speak English, that I
must run betwixt these ranks, and
that they would flog me all the way, as
I ran, and if I ran quick, it would be so
much the better, as they would quit when
I got to the end of the ranks. There
appeared to be a general rejoicing
around me, yet, I could find nothing like
joy in my breast; but I started to the
race with all the resolution and vigor I
was capable of exerting, and found that
it was as I had been told, for I was
flogged the whole way. When I had got
near the end of the lines, I was struck
with something that appeared to me to be
a stick, or the handle of a tommahawk,
which caused me to fall to the ground.
On my recovering my senses, I
endeavored to renew my race: but as I
arose, some one cast sand in my eyes,
which blinded me so, that I could not
see where to run. They continued beating

Betwixt these ranks—
Nearly all male captives
were compelled to run the
gauntlet—a combina-
tion of torture, a test of
courage, and an initiation.
Not many captives were
forced to run the gaunt-
let more than once. Men
who made a bold run
usually came off better
than those who were fear-
ful of the ordeal because
the Indians admired cour-
age. Smith received a
severe beating because
of the large number of
Indian warriors gathered
at Fort Duquesne await-
ing Braddock's army—
probably four or five
hundred.

Men were sometimes
beaten to death when
running the gauntlet. The
severity of the treatment
captives received de-
pended largely on the
temper of the Indians at
the time.

me most intolerably, until I was at length insensible; but before I lost my senses, I remember my wishing them to strike the fatal blow, for I thought they intended killing me, but apprehended they were too long about it.

The first thing I remember was my being in the fort, amidst the French and Indians, and a French doctor standing by me, who had opened a vein in my left arm: after which, the interpreter asked me how I did, I told him I felt much pain; the doctor then washed my wounds, and the bruised places of my body, with French brandy. As I felt faint, and the brandy smelt well, I asked for some inwardly, but the doctor told me, by the interpreter, that it did not suit my case.

When they found I could speak, a number of Indians came around me, and examined me, with threats of cruel death, if I did not tell the truth. The first question they asked me, was, how many men were there in the party that were coming from Pennsylvania, to join Braddock? I told them the truth, that there were three hundred. The next question was, were they well armed? I told them they were all well armed, (meaning the arm of flesh) for they had only about thirty guns among the whole of them; which, if the Indians had known, they would certainly have gone and cut them all off; therefore, I could not in conscience let them know the defenceless situation of these road-cutters. I was then sent to the hospital, and carefully attended by the doctors,

Open a vein — Blood-letting, a common medical practice of the time, was still praised some forty years later by Dr. Benjamin Rush because: "It removes or lessens pain in every part of the body, and more especially in the head. . . . In dislocations of bones which resist both skill and force, it has been suggested that bleeding, until fainting is induced, would produce such a relaxation in the muscles as to favour their reduction."

and recovered quicker than what I
expected.

Some time after I was there, I was
visited by the Delaware Indian already
mentioned, who was at the taking of me,
and could speak some English. Though
he spoke but bad English, yet I found him
to be a man of considerable under-
standing. I asked him if I had done any
thing that had offended the Indians, which
caused them to treat me so unmercifully?
He said no, it was only an old custom the
Indians had, and it was like how do you
do; after that he said I would be well
used. I asked hm if I should be admitted
to remain with the French? He said no
—and told me that as soon as I recovered,
I must not only go with the Indians, but
must be made an Indian myself. I asked
him what news from Braddock's army?
He said the Indians spied them every day,
and he showed me by making marks on
the ground with a stick, that Braddock's
army was advancing in very close order,
and that the Indians would surround
them, take trees, and (as he expressed it)
<u>shoot um down all one pigeon.</u>

Shortly after this, on the 9th day of July
1755, in the morning I heard a great stir
in the fort. As I could then walk with a
staff in my hand, I went out of the door
which was just by the wall of the fort,
and stood upon the wall and viewed the
Indians in a huddle before the gate, where
were the barrels of powder, bullets,
flints &c. and every one taking what
suited; I saw the Indians also march off
in rank, intire—likewise the French
Canadians, and some regulars, after

Take trees—Smith means
to take cover or hide be-
hind trees, which is the
most common and best
way to fight in the woods.

viewing the Indians and French in different positions, I computed them to be about four hundred, and wondered that they attempted to go out against Braddock with so small a party. I was then in high hopes that I would soon see them fly before the British troops, and that general Braddock would take the fort and rescue me.

I remained anxious to know the event of this day; and in the afternoon I again observed a great noise and commotion in the fort, and though at that time I could not understand French, yet I found that it was the voice of Joy and triumph, and feared that they had received what I called bad news.

I had observed some of the old country soldiers speak Dutch, as I spoke Dutch I went to one of them, and asked him, what was the news? he told me that a runner had just arrived, who said that Braddock would certainly be defeated; that the Indians and French had surrounded him, and were concealed behind trees and in gullies, and kept a constant fire upon the English, and that they saw the English falling in heaps, and if they did not take the river which was the only gap, and make their escape, there would not be one man left alive before sun down. Some time after this I heard a number of scalp halloo's and saw a company of Indians and French coming in. I observed they had a great many bloody scalps, grenadiers' caps, British canteens, bayonets &c. with them. They brought the news that Braddock was defeated. After that, another company

**Dutch** — Here Dutch refers to Pennsylvania Dutch, a dialect of High German.

**The Indians and French** —Captain Beaujeu of Fort Duquesne is credited with leading the Indians and some French troops in the ambush and attack on General Braddock's army. The fight took place July 9, 1755, at a ford on the Monongahela River some ten miles above the fort. Beaujeu was killed early in the fight but his attack resulted in the defeat and rout of Braddock's force.

came in, which appeared to be about
one hundred, and chiefly Indians, and it
seemed to me that almost every one of this
company was carrying scalps; after this
came another company with a number of
waggon-horses, and also a great many
scalps. Those that were coming in, and
those that had arrived, kept a constant
firing of small arms, and also the great
guns in the fort, which were
accompanied with the most hedious
shouts and yells from all quarters; so
that it appeared to me as if the infernal
regions had broke loose.

About sun down I beheld a small party
coming in with about a dozen prisoners,
stripped naked, with their hands tied
behind their backs, and their faces and
part of their bodies blacked—these
prisoners they burned to death on the
bank of Alegheny River opposite to the
fort. I stood on the fort wall until I beheld
them begin to burn one of these men,
they had him tied to a stake, and kept
touching him with fire-brands, red-hot
irons &c. and he screeming in a most
doleful manner,—the Indians in the
mean time yelling like infernal spirits.
As this scene appeared too shocking for
me to behold, I retired to my lodgings
both sore and sorry.

When I came into my longings I saw
Russel's Seven Sermons, which they had
brought from the field of battle, which a
Frenchman made a present of to me.
From the best information I could receive
there were only seven Indians and four
French killed in this battle, and five
hundred British lay dead in the field;

**Russel's Seven Sermons**
—This book by Robert
Russel was originally
published in London c.
1700; later it was re-
printed there and in
America fifty-two times.

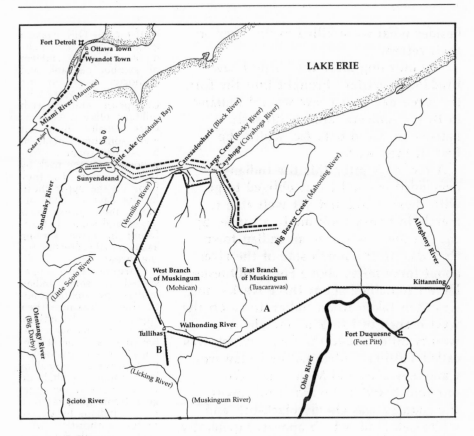

## Map 2

besides what were killed in the river on their retreat.

The morning after the battle I saw Braddock's artilery brought into the fort, the same day I also saw several Indians in British-officers' dress with sash, half-moon, laced hats &c. which the British then wore.

A few days after this the Indians demanded me and I was obliged to go with them. I was not yet well able to march, but they took me in a canoe, up the Alegheny River to an Indian town that was on the north side of the river, about forty miles above Fort DuQuesne. Here I remained about three weeks, and was then taken to an Indian town on the west branch of Muskingum, about twenty miles above the forks, which was called Tullihas, inhabited by Delawares, Caughnewagos and Mohicans.—On our rout betwixt the aforesaid towns, the country was chiefly black-oak and white-oak land, which appeared generally to be good wheat land, chiefly second and third rate, intermixed with some rich bottoms.

The day after my arrival at the aforesaid town, a number of Indians collected about me, and one of them began to pull the hair out of my head. He had some ashes on a piece of bark, in which he frequently dipped his fingers in order to take the firmer hold, and so he went on, as if he had been plucking a turkey, until he had all the hair clean out of my head, except a small spot about three or four inches square on my crown; this they cut off with a pair of scissors,

Half-moon—This was a gorget, a circular or half-moon shaped emblem or symbol of rank and authority worn in the eighteenth century by European and British military officers. Gorgets were usually silver but were sometimes made of brass or copper. Suspended from the neck by ribbons or cords, they hung on the upper chest. In the days of body armor, the gorget was larger and somewhat different in shape, serving as an actual protection for the throat.

Gorgets were presented to some Indian leaders by military authorities seeking their support and friendship. These Indians were referred to as "gorget captains." It was customary to engrave an animal or bird totem symbol on these presentation gorgets. Some gorgets given to the Indians by United States authorities were embossed with the figure of an eagle.

Indian Town—*The Kittanning villages, inhabited chiefly by Delawares. On September 8, 1756, fourteen months after Smith's compulsory visit, they were attacked and destroyed by the Provincial troops, under the command of Col. John Armstrong. Now the site of the flourishing town of Kittanning, the county seat of Armstrong county, Pennsylvania.*

**Tullihas** — Smith indicates that he and his captors traveled overland to the Ohio Indian town of Tullihas, located at or near where the Mohican and Owl Creek join to form the Walhonding. The "Great Trail" between Fort Duquesne and Detroit passed some miles to the north. From it the "Muskingum Trail" led south and struck the "Walhonding Trail" at Coshocton. The Walhonding Trail passed Tullihas, then ran southwest to the famous "Warriors' Path" in the Scioto Valley.

**Scissors** — The traders brought the Indians many items they could not make themselves: common objects and implements like scissors, knives, axes, needles, awls, brass or copper kettles, fish hooks, brass wire, hoes, metal tomahawks, and guns.

Because these items were very helpful to the Indians, they became dependent on the fur traders; unfortunately this diminished the self-sufficient Indian culture.

**Silver brooches** — These ornaments were made of sheet silver and traded in large quantities to the Indians by French and English fur traders. Made by silversmiths in Canada and the colonies, brooches were produced in a variety of sizes—from the size of a dime to three or four inches in diameter. Some were elaborately decorated with perforations in the shapes of

excepting three locks, which they dressed up in their own mode. Two of these they wraped round with a narrow beaded garter made by themselves for that purpose, and the other they platted at full length, and then stuck it full of silver broches. After this they bored my nose and ears, and fixed me off with ear rings and nose jewels, then they ordered me to strip off my clothes and put on a breech-clout, which I did; they then painted my head, face and body in various colours. They put a large belt of wampom on my neck, and silver bands on my hands and right arm; and so an old chief led me out in the street and gave the alarm halloo, <u>coo-wigh</u>, several times repeated quick, and on this all that were in the town came running and stood round the old chief, who held me by the hand in the midst.—As I at that time knew nothing of their mode of adoption, and had seen them put to death all they had taken, and as I never could find that they saved a man alive at Braddock's defeat, I made no doubt but they were about putting me to death in some cruel manner. The old chief holding me by the hand, made a long speech very loud, and when he had done he handed me to three young squaws, who led me by the hand down the bank into the river until the water was up to our middle. The squaws then made signs to me to plunge myself into the water, but I did not undertand them; I thought that the result of the council was that I should be drowned, and that these young ladies were to be the executioners. They all three laid violent hold of me, and I for some time opposed them with all my might, which occasioned loud laughter by the multitude that were on the bank of the river. At length one of the squaws made out to speak a little English (for I believe they began to be afraid of me) and said, <u>no hurt you</u>; on this I gave myself up to their ladyships, who were as good as their word; for though they plunged me under water, and washed and rubbed me severely, yet I could not say they hurt me much.

These young women then led me up to the council house, where some of the tribe were ready with new cloths for me. They gave me a new ruffled shirt, which I put on, also a pair of leggins done off with ribbons and beads, likewise a pair of mockasons, and garters dressed with beads, Porcupine-quills, and redhair— also a tinsel laced cappo. They again painted my head and face with various colors, and tied a bunch of red feathers to one of these locks they had left on the crown of my head, which stood up five or six inches. They seated me on a bear skin, and gave me a pipe, tomahawk, and polecat skin pouch, which had been skinned pocket fashion, and contained tobacco, killegenico, or dry sumach leaves, which they mix with their tobacco,—also spunk, flint and steel. When I was thus seated, the Indians came in dressed and painted in their grandest manner. As they came in they took their seats and for a considerable time there was a profound silence, every one was smoking,—but not a word was spoken among them.—At length one of

hearts, diamonds, triangles, and other designs.

Nose jewels and earrings were also made of silver. The nose jewel was a half-moon, or circular, ornament that fastened in the septum of the nose and hung on the upper lip.

Silversmiths and their assistants supplied thousands of these ornaments, as well as silver arm and wrist bands, rings, gorgets, and crosses to the fur traders every year. Such jewelry was popular until the late nineteenth century.

**Adoption by the Indians** —*John McCullough, a boy, who was captured by the Indians, near Fort Loudon, in 1756, underwent like transformation. He was painted, feathered, and ducked in the Allegheny river near Fort DuQuesne, then clad in a new ruffled shirt and told he had become an Indian.*

During the adoption ceremony Smith was ducked in the river to wash out his white blood. Thereafter he was no longer considered a white man, but truly an Indian.

Jonathan Alder—who was captured in Virginia in 1781 when he was eight—ran the gauntlet, was washed, and dressed in similar fashion.

However, not all captives underwent the same ritual. Some were adopted much more informally. Once adopted they seem to have been regarded by the Indians as brothers and no longer white.

**New ruffled shirt**—By the mid-eighteenth century

the Indians east of the Mississippi were wearing many articles of clothing that were also worn by white men. Cloth shirts, skirts, and leggings, and woolen blankets were all brought to the Indians by traders, or were available at the trading posts. While the Indians continued to use buckskin for moccasins, leggings, and some of their clothing, they found the European cloth to be superior for many uses.

Red hair — Deer, moose, horse, or porcupine hair—and sometimes locks of human hair—were dyed with vermillion ochre used for decoration by the Indians. Vermillion was obtained from the traders and used to color Indian faces, hair, and bodies.

Tomahawk—Metal tomahawks in a variety of forms were developed from belt axes, hatchets, and battle axes of ancient and medieval times. Manufactured in Europe, England, and America, tomahawks were distributed among most of the Indian tribes of North America.

When an iron or brass pipe bowl was added to the poll or head of the squaw axe, and the handle bored as a pipestem, it became a pipe-tomahawk, essentially a warrior's fighting weapon.

Since white men usually called all belt axes used by the Indians "tomahawks," it is not possible to determine what type Smith and his Indian relatives had.

the chiefs made a speech, which was delivered to me by an interpreter,—and was as followeth:—"My son, you are now flesh of our flesh, and bone of our bone. By the ceremony which was performed this day, every drop of white blood was washed out of your veins; you are taken into the Caughnewago nation, and initiated into a warlike tribe; you are adopted into a great family, and now received with great seriousness and solemnity in the room and place of a great man; after what has passed this day, you are now one of us by an old strong law and custom—My son, you have now nothing to fear, we are now under the same obligations to love, support and defend you, that we are to love and to defend one another, therefore you are to consider yourself as one of our people."—At this time I did not believe this fine speech, especially that of the white blood being washed out of me; but since that time I have found that there was much sincerity in said speech,—for, from that day I never knew them to make any distinction between me and themselves in any respect whatever until I left them.—If they had plenty of cloathing I had plenty, if we were scarce we all shared one fate.

After this ceremony was over, I was introduced to my new kin, and told that I was to attend a feast that evening, which I did. And as the custom was, they gave me also a bowl and wooden spoon, which I carried with me to the place, where there was a number of large brass kettles full of boiled venison and green corn;

Scoouwa at his adoption ceremony.

**Polecat** — This member of the weasel family was possibly a martin, fisher, or mink.

**In the room and place of a great man**—Many captives were adopted into Indian families to replace members killed in battle. Captives were expected to conduct themselves in a manner that would honor the memory of those persons. Some tribes, like the Iroquois, depended on captives to replace the warriors they lost in their numerous wars.

**Green corn**—These were young tender ears of Indian corn suitable for cooking.

**Pluggy**—*A Mohawk chief, styled Captain Pluggy (probably son of Tecanyaterighto) appeared at the council held by Lord Dunmore with the Indians at or near Fort Pitt, in the fall of 1774.*

*He became celebrated, leading many bloody forays into Western Pennsylvania, Virginia, and Kentucky. Patrick Henry, Governor of Virginia in 1777, authorized an expedition to be raised and directed exclusively against the "enemy of Pluggystown." It was abandoned, however, from the apprehension it might cause a general Indian war. . . .*

*Pluggy and his band defeated the whites near McClelland's Station, now Georgetown, Kentucky, on Christmas day, 1776, and again on Jan. 1, 1777. . . .*

*Indian towns were often known to the whites by the name of a prominent chief or warrior. "Pluggystown" was also known as Upper*

every one advanced with his bowl and spoon and had his share given him.— After this, one of the chiefs made a short speech, and then we began to eat.

The name of one of the chiefs in this town was Tecanyaterighto, alias Pluggy, and the other Asallecoa, alias Mohawk Solomon.—As Pluggy and his party were to start the next day to war, to the frontiers of Virginia, the next thing to be performed was the war dance, and their war songs. At their war dance they had both vocal and instrumental music. They has a short hollow gum close in one end, with water in it, and parchment stretched over the open end thereof, which they beat with one stick, and made a sound nearly like a muffled drum,—all those who were going on this expedition collected together and formed. An old Indian then began to sing, and timed the music by beating on this drum, as the ancients formerly timed their music by beating the tabor. On this the warriors began to advance, or move forward in concert, like well disciplined troops would march to the fife and drum. Each warrior had a tomahawk, spear or warmallet in his hand, and they all moved regularly towards the east, or the way they intended to go to war. At length they all stretched their tomahawks towards the Potomack, and giving a hideous shout or yell, they wheeled quick about, and danced in the same manner back. The next was the war song. In performing this, only one sung at a time, in a moving posture, with a tomahawk in his hand, while all the other wariors were engaged in calling aloud <u>he-uh</u>, <u>he-uh</u>, which they constantly repeated, while the war song was going on. When the warior that was singing had ended his song, he struck a war-post with his tomahawk, and with a loud voice told what warlike exploits he had done, and what he now intended to do: which were answered by the other wariors with loud shouts of applause. Some who had not before intended to go to war, at this time were so animated by this performance, that they took up the tomahawk and sung the war song which was answered with shouts of joy, as they were then initiated into the present marching company. The next morning this company all collected at one place, with their heads and faces painted with various colors, and packs upon their backs: they marched off, all silent, except the commander, who, in the front, sung the travelling song, which began in this manner: <u>hoo caugh-tainte heegana</u>. Just as the rear passed the end of the town, they began to fire in their slow manner, from the front to the rear, which was accompanied with shouts and yells from all quarters.

This evening I was invited to another sort of dance, which was a kind of promiscuos dance. The young men stood in one rank, and the young women in another, about one rod apart, facing each other. The one that raised the tune, or started the song, held a small gourd or dry shell of a squash, in his hand, which contained beads or small stones, which rattled. When he began to sing, he timed the tune with

*Chillicothe, . . . and as Old Chillicothe, four miles below Circleville, on the west side of the Scioto, where the celebrated Logan resided, and where he delivered his famous speech.*

Later research by John Bakeless disagrees with Darlington's comments. Bakeless has found that Pluggy had towns at different places in the Scioto Valley and the site of present day Delaware seems to have been his last town. Bakeless contends that Pluggy was killed December 29, 1776, while leading an attack on McClelland's Station in Kentucky.

his rattle; both men and women danced
and sung together, advancing towards
each other, stooping until their heads
would be touching together, and then
ceased from dancing, with loud shouts,
and retreated and formed again, and
so repeated the same thing over and over,
for three or four hours, without
intermission. This exercise appeared to
me at first, irrational and insipid; but
I found that in singing their tunes, they
used ya ne no hoo wa ne, &c. like our
fa sol la, and though they have no such
thing as jingling verse, yet they can
intermix sentences with their notes,
and say what they please to each other,
and carry on the tune in concert. I found
that this was a kind of wooing or courting
dance, and as they advanced stooping
with their heads together, they could
say what they pleased in each others ear,
without disconcerting their rough music,
and the others, or those near, not hear
what they say.

Shortly after this I went out to hunt,
in company with Mohawk Solomon,
some of the Caughnewagas, and a
Delaware Indian that was married to a
Caughnewaga squaw. We travelled about
south from this town, and the first night
we killed nothing, but we had with us
green corn, which we roasted and ate
that night. The next day we encamped
about twelve o'clock, and the hunters
turned out to hunt, and I went down the
run that we encamped on, in company
with some squaws and boys, to hunt
plumbs, which we found in great plenty.
On my return to camp I observed a

large piece of fat meat: the Delaware
Indian that could talk some English,
observed me looking earnestly at this
meat, and asked me <u>what meat you think
that is?</u> I said I supposed it was bear
meat; he laughed and said, <u>ho, all one
fool you, beal now elly pool</u>, and pointed
to the other side of the camp, he said
<u>look at that skin, you think that beal
skin?</u> I went and lifted the skin, which
appeared like an ox-hide: he then said,
<u>what skin you think that?</u> I replied, that
I thought it was a buffaloe hide; he
laughed and said <u>you fool again, you know
nothing, you think buffaloe that colo?</u> I
acknowledged I did not know much about
these things, and told him I never saw a
buffaloe, and that I had not heard what
color they were. He replyed <u>by and by you
shall see gleat many buffaloe: he now go
to gleat lick. That skin no buffaloe skin,
that skin buck-elk skin</u>. They went out
with horses, and brought in the remainder
of this buck-elk, which was the fattest
creature I ever saw of the tallow kind.

We remained at this camp about eight
or ten days, and killed a number of deer.
Though we had neither bread nor salt
at this time, yet we had both roast and
boiled meat in great plenty, and they
were frequently inviting me to eat, when
I had no appetite.

We then moved to the buffaloe lick,
where we killed several buffaloe, and in
their small brass kettles they made about
half a bushel of salt. I suppose this lick
was about thirty or forty miles from the
aforesaid town, and some where between
the Muskingum, Ohio and Sciota. About

Buffalo Lick—*In Licking and
Fairfield counties, now
known as the Reservoir or
Licking Summit of the Ohio
Canal, ten miles south of
Newark. The main Indian trail
from the forks of the Ohio to
the Miami towns led by this
swamp, then, no doubt, of vast
extent. Christopher Gist, agent*

*of the Ohio Company (of Virginia), sent out to examine the country, with George Croghan and Andrew Montour, messengers, with presents from Governor Hamilton, of Pennsylvania, to the Twightwees (Miamis), reached this point and encamped on January 17th, 1751. On the next day they "set out from the Great Swamp," as it is noticed by Gist in his journal.*

The buffalo lick which Smith estimates was some thirty to forty miles from Tullihas may have been in the vicinity of Buckeye Lake, now a residential and recreational area. The lake is located where Licking, Fairfield, and Perry counties come together.

At the time of Smith's captivity it was a large swamp, a relic of the glacial period. It was then about seven miles long and averaged three-quarters of a mile or more in width. In the center was a pond four to five hundred yards wide by five miles long. Elnathan Scofield's survey map dated 1801 shows the marsh as it would have appeared in Smith's day.

In the 1825-1837 period when levees were built along the west and north banks to impound the water for the canal, the open body of water was expanded to approximately 4,000 acres, the present area of Buckeye Lake.

It seems probable that the buffalo lick where Smith says the Indians made a half bushel of salt may have been the same salt lick Christopher

the lick was clear, open woods, and thin white-oak land, and at that time there were large roads leading to the lick, like waggon roads. We moved from this lick about six or seven miles, and encamped on a creek.

Though the Indians had given me a gun, I had not yet been admitted to go out from the camp to hunt. At this place Mohawk Solomon asked me to go out with him to hunt, which I readily agreed to. After some time we came upon some fresh buffaloe tracks. I had observed before this that the Indians were upon their guard, and afraid of an enemy; for, until now they and the southern nations had been at war. As we were following the buffaloe tracks, Solomon seemed to be upon his guard, went very slow, and would frequently stand and listen, and appeared to be in suspense. We came to where the tracks were very plain in the sand, and I said it was surely buffaloe tracks; he said, <u>hush, you know nothing, may be buffaloe tracks, may be Catawba</u>. He went very cautious until we found some fresh buffaloe dung: he then smiled and said, <u>Catawba cannot make so</u>. He then stopped, and told me an odd story about the Catawbas. He said, that formerly the Catawbas came near one of their hunting camps, and at some distance from the camp lay in ambush; and in order to decoy them out, sent two or three Catawbas in the night, past their camp, with buffaloe hoofs fixed on their feet, so as to make artificial tracks. In the morning those in the camp followed after these tracks, thinking they were Buffaloe, until they were fired on by the Catawbas, and several of them killed; the others fled, collected a party and pursed the Catawbas; but they, in their subtilty brought with them rattle-snake poison, which they had collected from the bladder that lieth at the root of the snakes' teeth; this they had corked up in a short piece of a cane-stalk; they had also brought with them small cane or reed, about the size of a rye straw, which they made sharp at the end like a pen, and dipped them in this poison, and stuck them in the ground among the grass, along their own tracks, in such a position that they might stick into the legs of the pursuers, which answered the design; and as the Catawbas had runners behind to watch the motion of the pursuers, when they found that a number of them were lame, being artificially snake bit, and that they were all turning back, the Catawbas turned upon the pursuers, and defeated them, and killed and scalped all those that were lame.—When Solomon had finished this story, and found that I understood him, concluded by saying, you don't know, Catawba velly bad Indian, Catawba all one Devil Catawba.

Some time after this, I was told to take the dogs with me and go down the creek, perhaps I might kill a turkey; it being in the afternoon, I was also told not to go far from the creek, and to come up the creek again to the camp, and to take care not to get lost. When I had gone some distance down the creek, I came upon fresh buffaloe tracks, and as I had a

Gist describes on the Licking River six miles above its mouth. This lick was probably fifteen or twenty miles east of the Great Swamp.

Catawbas—This warlike tribe inhabited the Carolinas, chiefly in the country adjacent to the Catawba river. They were the ancient and inveterate enemies of the Iroquois or Six Nations, with whom they were continually at war. The other tribes conceded to them the highest character for bravery, daring and subtlety. When South Carolina was first settled by the English, in 1670, the Catawbas could muster fifteen hundred warriors; in 1836, the entire tribe numbered less than one hundred, who occupied the fine tract of land, fifteen miles square, in the counties of York and Lancaster, which was originally reserved for them by the Proprietary Government. The few remaining of this once formidable nation now reside in the western part of North Carolina.

Some writers suppose that the Catawbas were the remnant of the celebrated Eries, who were expelled from their ancient country on the shores of Lake Erie and driven south by the conquering Iroquois, in 1650. There is considerable evidence in support of this view.

number of dogs with me to stop the
buffaloe, I concluded I would follow
after and kill one; and as the grass and
weeds were rank, I could readily follow
the track. A little before sundown I
despaired of coming up with them: I was
then thinking how I might get to camp
before night: I concluded as the buffaloe
had made several turns, if I took the track
back to the creek, it would be dark before
I could get to camp; therefore I thought
I would take a near way through the hills,
and strike the creek a little below the
camp; but as it was cloudy weather, and
I a very young woodsman, I could find
neither creek or camp. When night came
on I fired my gun several times, and
hallooed, but could have no answer.
The next morning early, the Indians were
out after me, and as I had with me ten
or a dozen dogs, and the grass and weeds
rank, they could readily follow my track.
When they came up with me, they
appeared to be in a very good humor.
I asked Solomon if he thought I was
running away, he said <u>no, no, you go too
much clooked</u>. On my return to camp
they took my gun from me, and for this
rash step I was reduced to a bow and
arrows, for near two years. We were
out on this tour for about six weeks.

This country is generally hilly, though
intermixed with considerable quantities
of rich upland, and some good bottoms.

When we returned to the town, Pluggy
and his party had arrived, and brought
with them a considerable number of
scalps and prisoners from the South
Branch of the Potomack: they also

South branch of the
Potomac—This body of
water lies in what is now
West Virginia.

brought with them an English Bible, which they gave to a Dutch woman who was a prisoner; but as she could not read English, she made a present of it to me, which was very acceptable.

I remained in this town until some time in October, when my adopted brother, called Tontileaugo, who had married a Wiandot squaw, took me with him to Lake Erie. We proceeded up west branch of Muskingum, and for some distance up the river the land was hilly but intermixed with large bodies of tolerable rich upland, and excellent bottoms. We proceeded on, to the head waters of the west branch of Muskingum. On the head waters of this branch, and from thence to the waters of Cansadooharie, there is a large body of rich, well lying land—the timber is ash, walnut, sugar-tree, buckeye, honey-locust, and cherry, intermixed with some oak, hickory, &c.—This tour was at the time that the blackhaws were ripe, and we were seldom out of sight of them: they were common here both in the bottoms and upland.

On this route we had no horses with us, and when we started from the town, all the pack I carried was a pouch, containing my books, a little dried venison, and my blanket. I had then no gun, but Tontileaugo, who was a first rate hunter, carried a rifle gun, and every day killed deer, racoons or bears. We left the meat, excepting a little for present use, and carried the skins with us until we encamped, and then stretched them with elm bark, in a frame made with poles

Canesadooharie—*The Black river, in Lorain county. The route of the Indians with Smith appears to have been from the town of Tullihas up along the lake fork of the Mohican creek to its source in the northern part of Ashland county; thence a few miles north-easterly to the head waters of Black river, in Lorain. On the map published by Lewis Evans, in 1755, the "Guahadahuri" is the only river laid down between the Cuyahoga and the Sandusky, although it is placed too far west—about the locality of the Vermillion. On Captain Thos. Hutchins' large map of 1778, Black river is correctly laid down, and named "Riviere en Grys" (Gray). . . . [Taylor] and others have been mislead by the misprint of eight (in all the editions of the narrative excepting the original and the present) instead of eighty miles, stated by Smith to be about the distance between the Sandusky and Black rivers. The correct distance does not exceed fifty-two miles.*

*The Falls of Black river, at Elyria, in Lorain county, are doubtless the same mentioned in the Narrative; their descent is forty feet perpendicular. The reader will, of course, make due allowance for the errors in the distances given in the Narrative. Smith was young, and his means of taking and preserving notes, either in the wigwam or the canoe, very scanty.*

Haws — This refers to hawthorn berries.

Rifle gun — Most of the firearms used by Indians at this time were smooth-bore flintlock trade guns or fowling pieces obtained from the traders in exchange for furs. Military muskets, which were also smoothbore, were issued to the Indians by English or French forces who sought their support in wartime.

Many Indians preferred the smoothbore trade guns to muskets because they were lightweight and easier to load. Loaded with shot they served as fowling pieces used for shooting birds or small animals; when loaded with a ball they were powerful enough for use in warfare, or to shoot bear, deer, elk, or buffalo.

Rifles, or rifled guns as they were commonly described, were the favorite weapons of American frontiersmen. The spiral grooves cut into the bores of these guns made them superior to smoothbore guns in range and accuracy. The American long rifle was largely the product of Pennsylvania gunsmiths, although it came to be called almost universally the "Kentucky rifle." It was the most accurate rifle of its time.

stuck in the ground and tied together with lynn or elm bark; and when the skins were dried by the fire, we packed them up, and carried them with us the next day.

As Tontileaugo could not speak English, I had to make use of all the Caughnewaga I had learned even to talk very imperfectly with him: but I found I learned to talk Indian faster this way, than when I had those with me who could speak English.

As we proceeded down the Canesadooharie waters, our packs increased by the skins that were daily killed, and became so very heavy that we could not march more than eight or ten miles per day. We came to Lake Erie about six miles west of the mouth of Canesadooharie. As the wind was very high the evening we came to the Lake, I was surprized to hear the roaring of the water, and see the high waves that dashed against the shore, like the Ocean. We encamped on a run near the lake; and as the wind fell that night, the next morning the lake was only in a moderate motion, and we marched on the sand along the side of the water, frequently resting ourselves, as we were heavy laden. I saw on the strand a number of large fish, that had been left in flat or hollow places; as the wind fell and the waves abated, they were left without water, or only a small quantity; and numbers of Bald and Grey Eagles, &c. were along the shore devouring them.

Some time in the afternoon we came to a large camp of Wiandots, at the mouth

of Canesadooharie, where Tontileaugo's
wife was. Here we were kindly received:
they gave us a kind of rough, brown
potatoes, which grew spontaneously and
is called by the Caughnewagas <u>ohnenata</u>.
These potatoes peeled and dipped in
racoons' fat, taste nearly like our sweet-
potatoes. They also gave us what they
call <u>caneheanta</u>, which is a kind of
homony, made of green corn, dried,
and beans mixed together.

From the head waters of Canesadooharie
to this place, the land is generally good;
chiefly first or second rate, and,
comparatively, little or no third rate.
The only refuse is some swamps, that
appear to be too wet for use, yet I
apprehend that a number of them, if
drained, would make excellent meadows.
The timber is black-oak, walnut, hickory,
cherry, black-ash, white-ash, water-ash,
buckeye, black-locust, honey-locust,
sugar-tree, and elm: there is also some
land, though, comparatively, but small,
where the timber is chiefly white-oak,
or beach—this may be called third rate.
In the bottoms, and also many places
in the upland, there is a large quantity
of wild apple, plumb, and red and
black-haw trees. It appeared to be well
watered, and a plenty of meadow ground,
intermixed with upland, but no large
prairies or glades, that I saw or heard
of. In this route, deer, bear, turkeys, and
racoons, appeared plenty, but no
buffaloe, and very little sign of elks.

We continued our camp at the mouth of
Canesadooharie for some time, where
we killed some deer, and a great many

The timber is black-oak
—Like the surveyors who
would later enter this region, throughout his jour-
neys Smith evaluated the
fertility of various regions
according to the timber
growing there. Trees were
regarded as good soil in-
dicators;     nut-bearing
trees, for example, indi-
cated superior—or first
rate—soil.

**Birchbark canoes** — Used in the Great Lakes region, these canoes ranged from about twelve or fourteen feet in length to large cargo canoes such as Smith describes. These might have had six or seven men paddling on each side and carried a total load of several tons.

Most large bark canoes were built in the lake country and in Canada. Some of the finest canoe makers were Ojibway and Cree Indians. These Algonquian people lived in the Great Lakes country and sometimes traded their products to other tribes who lived south of them.

Bark from the paper birch was the finest material for building canoes. Rolls of it were traded to Indians who lived where the birch did not grow. Canoes were also made from the bark of the elm, chestnut, basswood, hickory, spruce, and cottonwood. However, none of these could equal the qualities of the paper birch for excellence. The chief disadvantage of the bark canoe was its fragile nature. Easily damaged on rocks or snags, it had to be repaired frequently by doping the seams with a mixture of spruce gum, tallow, and charcoal.

racoons; the racoons here were remarkably large and fat.—At length we all embarked in a large birch bark canoe. This vessel was about four feet wide, and three feet deep, and about five and thirty feet long: and tho it could carry a heavy burden, it was so artfully and curiously constructed that four men could cary it several miles, or from one landing place to another, or from the waters of the Lake to the waters of the Ohio.—We proceeded up Canesadooharie a few miles and went on shore to hunt; but to my great surprise they carried the vessel that we all came in up the bank, and inverted it or turned the bottom up, and converted it to a dwelling house, and kindled a fire before us to warm ourseves by and cook. With our baggage and ourselves in this house we were very much crouded, yet our little house turned off the rain very well.

We kept moving and hunting up this river until we came to the falls; here we remained some weeks, and killed a number of deer, several bears, and a great many racoons. From the mouth of this river to the falls is about five and twenty miles. On our passage up I was not much out from the river, but what I saw was good land, and not hilly.

About the falls is thin chesnut land, which is almost the only chesnut timber I ever saw in this country.

While we remained here, I left my pouch with my books in camp, wrapt up in my blanket, and went out to hunt chesnuts. On my return to camp my books were missing. I enquired after them, and

asked the Indians if they knew where
they were, they told me that they
supposed the puppies had carried them
off. I did not believe them; but thought
they were displeased at my poring over
my books, and concluded that they had
destroyed them, or put them out of my
way.

After this I was again out after nuts,
and on my return beheld a new erection,
which were two white oak saplings, that
were forked about twelve feet high, and
stood about fifteen feet apart. They had
cut these saplings at the forks and laid
a strong pole across which appeared
in the form of a gallows, and the poles
they had shaved very smooth and painted
in places with vermillion. I could not
conceive the use of this piece of work,
and at length concluded it was a gallows,
I thought that I had displeased them
by reading my books, and that they
were about puting me to death.—The
next morning I observed them bringing
their skins all to this place and hanging
them over this pole, so as to preserve
them from being injured by the weather,
this removed my fears. They also buried
their large canoe in the ground, which
is the way they took to praserve this
sort of a canoe in the winter season.

As we had at this time no horses, every
one got a pack on his back, and we
steered an east course about twelve miles,
and encamped. The next morning we
proceeded on the same course about ten
miles to a large creek that empties into
Lake Erie betwixt Canesadooharie,
and Cayahaga. Here they made their

Large Creek—*Rocky river
in Medina, Lorain and Cuyahoga counties. According to
the distances given in the
narrative their "winter cabin"
was probably erected on the
east branch of the Rocky river,
either in the present township
of Hinckley in Medina county
or in the adjoining township
of Royalton in Cuyahoga.
Bear, deer and wolves were
very abundant in this region
so late as the year 1818.*

wintercabbin, in the following form.
They cut logs about fifteen feet long, and
laid these longs upon each other, and
drove posts in the ground at each end to
keep them together; the posts they tied
together at the top with bark, and by
this means raised a wall fifteen feet long,
and about four feet high, and in the same
manner they raised another wall
opposite to this, at about twelve feet
distance; then they drove forks in the
ground in the centre of each end, and
laid a strong pole from end to end on
these forks; and from these walls to the
poles, they set up poles instead of rafters,
and on these they tied small poles in place

Lynn—This refers to the     of laths; and a cover was made of lynn
linden tree.                bark which will run even in the winter
season.

As every tree will not run, they examine
the tree first, by trying it near the ground,
and when they find it will do, they fall
the tree and raise the bark with the
tomahawk, near the top of the tree about
five or six inches broad, then put the
tomahawk handle under this bark, and
pull it along down to the butt of the tree;
so that some times one piece of bark
will be thirty feet long; this bark they
cut at suitable lengths in order to cover
the hut.

At the end of these walls they set up
split timber, so that they had timber all
round, excepting a door at each end.
At the top, in place of a chimney, they
left an open place, and for bedding they
laid down the aforesaid kind of bark, on
which they spread bear skins. From
end to end of this hut along the middle

there were fires, which the squaws made
of dry split wood, and the holes or open
places that appeared, the squaws stopped
with moss, which they collected from
old logs; and at the door they hung a bear
skin; and notwithstanding the winters
are hard here, our lodging was much
better than what I expected.

It was some time in December when we
finished this winter cabin; but when we
had got into this comparatively fine
lodging, another difficulty arose, we had
nothing to eat. While I was travelling
with Tontileaugo, as was before
mentioned, and had plenty of fat
venison, bears meat and racoons, I
then thought it was hard living without
bread or Salt; but now I began to
conclude, that if I had any thing that
would banish pinching hunger, and keep
soul and body together I would be
content.

While the hunters were all out,
exerting themselves to the utmost of
their ability, the squaws and boys (in
which class I was) were scattered out in
the bottoms, hunting red-haws, black-haws
and hickory-nuts. As it was too late in
the year, we did not succeed in gathering
haws; but we had tolerable success in
scratching up hickory-nuts from under a
light snow, which we carried with us lest
the hunters should not succeed. After our
return the hunters came in, who had
killed only two small turkeys, which were
but little among eight hunters, and
thirteen squaws, boys, and children;—
but they were divided with the greatest
equity and justice—every one got their

equal share.

The next day the hunters turned out again, and killed one deer and three bears.

One of the bears was very large and remarkably fat. The hunters carried in meat sufficient to give us all a hearty supper and breakfast.

The squaws and all that could carry turned out to bring in meat,—every one had their share assigned them, and my load was among the least; yet, not being accustomed to carrying in this way, I got exceeding weary, and told them my load was too heavy, I must leave part of it and come for it again. They made a halt and only laughed at me, and took part of my load and added it to a young squaw's, who had as much before as I carried.

This kind of reproof had a greater tendency to excite me to exert myself in carrying without complaining, than if they had whipped me for laziness. After this the hunters held a council, and concluded that they must have horses to carry their loads; and that they would go to war even in this inclement season, in order to bring in horses.

Tontileaugo wished to be one of those who should go to war; but the votes went against him, as he was one of our best hunters; it was thought necessary to leave him at this winter camp to provide for the squaws and children; it was agreed upon that Tontileaugo and three others should stay, and hunt, and the other four go to war.

They then began to go through their

Votes went against him —Smith is using a figure of speech here. Tontileaugo was apparently urged to stay and care for the women and children as he was one of the most reliable hunters in the village. It seems doubtful that the "voting" was done formally.

Most serious problems in the tribal community were discussed and resolved by a council of men, and sometimes women, who were known for their wisdom and good judgment. Tecaughretanego, Smith's older brother, was such a leader because of his reasoning ability.

common ceremony. They sung their war
songs danced their war dances &c. And
when they were equipped they went off
singing their marching song, and firing
their guns. Our camp appeared to be
rejoicing; but I was grieved to think that
some innocent persons would be
murdered not thinking of danger.

After the departure of these warriors
we had hard times; and tho we were not
altogether out of provisions, we were
brought to short allowance. At length
Tontileaugo had considerable success;
and we had meat brought into camp
sufficient to last ten days. Tontileaugo then
took me with him in order to encamp
some distance from this winter cabbin,
to try his luck there. We carried no
provision with us, he said we would leave
what was there for the squaws and
children, and that we could shift for
ourselves. We steered about a south
course up the waters of this creek, and
encamped about ten or twelve miles from
the winter cabbin. As it was still cold
weather and a crust upon the snow,
which made a noise as we walked and
alarmed the deer, we could kill nothing,
and consequently went to sleep without
supper. The only chance we had under
these circumstances, was to hunt bear
holes; as the bears about Christmas
search out a winter lodging place, where
they lie about three or four months
without eating or drinking.—This may
appear to some incredible; but it is now
well known to be the case, by those who
live in the remote western parts of North
America.

The next morning early we proceeded on, and when we found a tree scratched by the bears climbing up, and the hole in the tree sufficiently large for the reception of the bear, we then fell a sapling or small tree, against or near the hole; and it was my business to climb up and drive out the bear, while Tontileaugo stood ready with his gun and bow. We went on in this manner until evening, without success; at length we found a large elm scratched, and a hole in it about forty feet up; but no tree nigh, suitable to lodge against the hole. Tontileaugo got a long pole and some dry rotten wood which he tied in bunches, with bark, and as there was a tree that grew near the elm, and extended up near the hole; but leaned the wrong way; so that we could not lodge it to advantage; but to remedy this inconvenience, he climed up this tree and carried with him his rotten wood, fire and pole. The rotten wood he tied to his belt, and to one end of the pole he tied a hook, and a piece of rotten wood which he set fire to, as it would retain fire almost like spunk; and reached this hook from limb to limb as he went up; when he got up, with this pole he put dry wood on fire into the hole, after he put in the fire he heard the bear snuff and he came speedily down, took his gun in his hand, and waited until the bear would come out; but it was some time before it appeared, and when it did appear, he attempted taking sight with his rifle; but it being then too dark, to see the sights, he set it down by a tree, and instantly bent his bow, took hold

of an arrow, and shot the bear a little
behind the shoulder; I was preparing also
to shoot an arrow, but he called to me to
stop, there was no occasion; and with
that the bear fell to the ground.

Being very hungry we kindled a fire,
opened the bear, took out the liver, and
wrapped some of the caul fat round and
put it on a wooden spit which we stuck
in the ground by the fire to roast, we then
skinned the bear, got on our kettle, and
had both roast and boiled, and also sauce
to our meat, which appeared to me to be
delicate fare. After I was fully satisfied I
went to sleep, Tontileaugo awoke me,
saying, come eat hearty, we have got
meat plenty now.

The next morning we cut down a lynn
tree, peeled bark and made a snug little
shelter, facing the south east, with a large
log betwixt us and the north west; we
made a good fire before us, and
scaffolded up our meat at one side.—
When we had finished our camp we went
out to hunt, searched two trees for bears,
but to no purpose. As the snow thawed a
little in the afternoon Tontileaugo killed
a deer, which we carried with us to camp.

The next day we turned out to hunt,
and near the camp we found a tree well
scratched; but the hole was above forty
feet high, and no tree that we could lodge
against the hole; but finding that it was
very hollow, we concluded that we would
cut down the tree with our tomahawks,
which kept us working a considerable
part of the day. When the tree fell we
ran up, Tontileaugo with his gun and
bow, and I with my bow ready bent.

Tontileaugo shot the bear through with his rifle, a little behind the shoulders; I also shot, but too far back; and not being then much accustomed to the business, my arrow penetrated only a few inches thro the skin. Having killed an old she bear and three cubs, we hawled her on the snow to the camp, and only had time afterwards, to get wood, make a fire, cook &c. before dark.

Early the next morning we went to business, searched several trees, but found no bears. On our way home we took three racoons out of a hollow elm, not far from the ground.

We remained here about two weeks, and in this time killed four bears, three deer, several turkeys, and a number of racoons. We packed up as much meat as we could carry, and returned to our winter cabin. On our arrival, there was great joy, as they were all in a starving condition,— the three hunters that we had left having killed but very little.—All that could carry a pack repaired to our camp to bring in meat.

Some time in February the four warriors returned, who had taken two scalps and six horses from the frontiers, of Pennsylvania. The hunters could then scatter out a considerable distance from the winter cabin, and encamp, kill meat and pack it in upon horses; so that we commonly after this had plenty of provision.

In this month we began to make sugar. As some of the elm bark will strip at this season, the squaws, after finding a tree that would do, cut it down, and with a crooked stick broad and sharp at the end, took the bark off the tree, and of this bark, made vessels in a curious manner, that would hold about two gallons each: they made above one hundred of these kind of vessels. In the sugar-tree they cut a notch, slooping down, and at the end of the notch, stuck in a tomahawk; in the place where they stuck the tomahawk, they drove a long chip, in order to carry the water out from the tree, and under this they set their vessel to receive it. As sugar trees were plenty and large here, they seldom or never notched a tree that was not two or three feet over. They also made bark vessels for carrying the water, that would hold about four gallons each. They had two brass kettles, that held about fifteen gallons each, and other smaller kettles in which they boiled the water. But as they could not at all times boil away the water as fast as it was collected, they made vessels of bark, that would hold about one hundred gallons each, for retaining the water; and tho' the sugar trees did not run every day, they had always a sufficient quantity of water to keep them boiling during the whole sugar season.

The way that we commonly used our sugar while encamped, was by putting it in bears fat until the fat was almost as sweet as the sugar itself, and in this we dipped our roasted venison. About this time some of the Indian lads and myself, were employed in making and attending traps for catching racoons, foxes, wild cats, &c.

As the racoon is a kind of water animal,

Maple sugar—Sugar was an important part of the diet of the Woodland Indians, who used iarge quantities of sugar, and disposed of the surplus to the traders. Alexander Henry, a white man living with a small band of Chippewa Indians in the Great Lakes country, recorded that they made 1,600 pounds of sugar during the spring of 1763.

In the 1830s when the Ohio Wyandots were facing the problem of removal west of the Mississippi, one of their objections was an absence of sugar maples in the area where they were to move.

that frequents the runs, or small water
courses, almost the whole night, we
made our traps on the runs, by laying
one small sapling on another, and driving
in posts to keep them from rolling. The
upper sapling we raised about eighteen
inches, and set so, that on the racoon's
touching a string, or small piece of
bark, the sapling would fall and kill it;
and lest the racoon should pass by, we
laid brush on both sides of the run, only
leaving the channel open.

The fox traps we made nearly in the
same manner, at the end of a hollow log,
or opposite to a hole at the root of a hollow
tree, and put venison on a stick for bait:
we had it so set that when the fox took
hold of the meat, the trap fell. While
the squaws were employed in making
sugar, the boys and men were engaged
in hunting and trapping.

About the latter end of March we began
to prepare for moving into town, in order
to plant corn: the squaws were then
frying the last of their bears fat, and
making vessels to hold it: the vessels were
made of deer skins, which were skinned
by pulling the skin off the neck, without
ripping. After they had taken off the
hair, they gathered it in small plaits round
the neck and with a string drew it together
like a purse: in the centre a pin was put,
below which they tied a string, and
while it was wet they blew it up like a
bladder, and let it remain in this manner,
until it was dry, when it appeared nearly
in the shape of a sugar loaf, but more
rounding at the lower end. One of these
vessels would hold about four or five

gallons; in these vessels it was they
carried their bears oil.

When all things were ready we moved
back to the falls of Canesadooharie. In
this route the land is chiefly first and
second rate, but too much meadow
ground, in proportion to the up land. The
timber is white ash, elm, black-oak,
cherry, buckeye, sugar-tree, lynn,
mulberry, beech, white-oak, hickory, wild
apple-tree, red-haw, black-haw, and
spicewood bushes. There is in some
places, spots of beech timber, which
spots may be called third rate land.
Buckeye, sugar-tree and spicewood, are
common in the woods here. There is in
some places, large swamps too wet for
any use.

On our arrival at the falls, (as we had
brought with us on horse back, about
two hundred weight of sugar, a large
quantity of bears oil, skins &c.) the canoe
we had buried was not sufficient to carry
all; therefore we were obliged to make
another one of elm bark. While we lay
here, a young Wiandot found my books:
on this they collected together; I was a
little way from the camp, and saw the
collection, but did not know what it
meant. They called me by my Indian
name, which was Scoouwa, repeatedly.
I ran to see what was the matter, they
showed me my books, and said they were
glad they had been found, for they knew I
was grieved at the loss of them, and that
they now rejoiced with me because they
were found. As I could then speak
some Indian, especially Caughnewaga
(for both that and the Wiandot tongue

Books—The incident of the finding of Smith's packet of books marked a turning point in his relationship with the Indians: Smith began to regard the Indians more frequently as individual humans. The shocking tortures he witnessed at Fort Duquesne he never forgot, but this was a time in which cruelty was commonplace. The so-called civilized nations also practiced burning, branding, mutilating, whipping, and various forms of execution.

As a rule, young children taken captive adapted much more easily to the Indian life. Some became completely "Indianized" and had no desire to return to their former lives. Older captives might live with the Indians for years but usually chose to return home when they were able to do so.

were spoken in this camp) I told them that I thanked them for the kindness they had always shown to me, and also for finding my books. They asked if the books were damaged? I told them not much. They then showed how they lay, which was in the best manner to turn off the water. In a deer skin pouch they lay all winter. The print was not much injured, though the binding was.—This was the first time that I felt my heart warm towards the Indians. Though they had been exceedingly kind to me, I still before detested them, on account of the barbarity I beheld after Braddock's defeat. Neither had I ever before pretended kindness, or expressed myself in a friendly manner; but I began now to excuse the Indians on account of their want of information.

When we were ready to embark, Tontileaugo would not go to town, but go up the river and take a hunt. He asked me if I choosed to go with him? I told him I did. We then got some sugar, bears oil bottled up in a bear's gut, and some dry venison, which we packed up, and went up Canesadooharie, about thirty miles, and encamped. At this time I did not know either the day of the week, or the month; but I supposed it to be about the first of April. We had considerable success in our business. We also found some stray horses, or a horse, mare, and a young colt; and though they had run in the woods all winter, they were in exceeding good order. There is plenty of grass here all winter, under the snow, and horses accustomed to the woods can work

it out.—These horses had run in the woods
until they were very wild.

Tontileaugo one night concluded that
we must run them down. I told him I
thought we could not accomplish it. He
said he had run down bears, buffaloes and
elks: and in the great plains, with only a
small snow on the ground, he had run
down a deer; and he thought that in one
whole day, he could tire, or run down any
four footed animal except a wolf. I
told him that though a deer was the
swiftest animal to run a short distance,
yet it would tire sooner than a horse.
He said he would at all events try the
experiment. He had heard the Wiandots
say, that I could run well, and now he
would see whether I could or not. I told
him that I never had run all day, and of
course was not accustomed to that way of
running. I never had run with the
Wiandots, more than seven or eight
miles at one time. He said that was
nothing, we must either catch these
horses, or run all day.

In the morning early we left camp,
and about sunrise we started after them,
striped naked excepting breech-clouts and
mockasons. About ten o'clock I lost
sight of both Tontileaugo and the horses,
and did not see them again until about
three o'clock in the afternoon. As the
horses run all day, in about three or four
miles square, at length they passed
where I was, and I fell in close after them.
As I then had a long rest, I endeavored
to keep a head of Tontileaugo, and after
some time I could hear him after me
calling <u>chakoh</u>, <u>chakoanaugh</u>, which

signifies, pull away or do your best. We pursued on, and after some time Tontileaugo passed me, and about an hour before sundown, we despaired of catching these horses and returned to camp where we had left our clothes.

I reminded Tontileaugo of what I had told him; he replied he did not know what horses could do. They are wonderful strong to run; but withal we made them very tired. Tontileaugo then concluded, he would do as the Indians did with wild horses, when out at war: which is to

**Shoot them through the neck**—This neck shot on horses was known as "grazing," which required very precise shooting at close range to accomplish successfully. A good percentage of the time the ball struck too low, killing the horse.

shoot them through the neck under the mane, and above the bone, which will cause them to fall and lie until they can halter them, and then they recover again. This he attemped to do; but as the mare was very wild, he could not get sufficiently nigh to shoot her in the proper place; however he shot, the ball passed too low, and killed her. As the horse and colt stayed at this place, we caught the horse, and took him and the colt with us to camp.

We stayed at this camp about two weeks, and killed a number of bears, racoons, and some beavers. We made a canoe of elm bark, and Tontileaugo embarked in it. He arrived at the falls that night; whilst I, mounted on horse back, with a bear skin saddle, and bark stirrups, proceeded by land to the falls: I came there the next morning, and we carried our canoe and loading past the falls.

The river is very rapid for some distance above the falls, which are about twelve or fifteen feet nearly perpendicular.

This river, called Canesadooharie,
interlocks with the West Branch of
Muskingum, runs nearly a north course,
and empties into the south side of Lake
Erie, about eighty miles east from
Sandusky, or betwixt Sandusky and
Cayahaga.

On this last route the land is nearly
the same, as that last described, only there
is not so much swampy or wet ground.

We again proceeded towards the lake, I
on horse back, and Tontileaugo by
water. Here the land is generally good,
but I found some difficulty in getting round
swamps and ponds. When we came to the
lake I proceeded along the strand, and
Tontileaugo near the shore, sometimes
paddling and sometimes polling his
canoe along.

After some time the wind arose, and he
went into the mouth of a small creek and
encamped. Here we staid several days on
account of high wind, which raised the
lake in great billows. While we were here
Tontileaugo went out to hunt, and when
he was gone a Wiandot came to our
camp; I gave him a shoulder of venison
which I had by the fire well roasted, and
he received it gladly, told me he was
hungry, and thanked me for my kindness.
When Tontileaugo came home, I told
him that a Wiandot had been at camp,
and that I gave him a shoulder of roasted
venison: he said that was very well, and
I suppose you gave him also sugar and
bears oil, to eat with his venison. I
told him I did not; as the sugar and bears
oil was down in the canoe I did not go for
it. He replied you have behaved just like

The Lake—*The color of the water is also noticed by the German Prince Maximilian of Wied in his book of travels in North America in 1833: "Lake Erie. The splendid bluish-green waters of which, like all the great Canadian lakes, are exactly of the same color as those of Switzerland."*

Sunyendeand—*Sir William Johnson, on his way home from Detroit in September, 1761, crossed the Portage from the mouth of the river at the site of the present town of Port Clinton. He then went down the Bay to "the encampment" "where the block-house is to be built," about the location of Venice, three miles west of Sandusky City. He mentions a Wyandot town as "almost opposite the Carrying-place," and "another village of Hurons about three miles distant" from the place of encampment.*

*[J. M. Root suggests] Smith's description of the locality of this town "can only apply to Pipe creek, and the big fields lying south-east of and about a mile and a half from the present town of Sandusky." . . . "Junqueindundeh" is the name given to an Indian village near the mouth of the Sandusky river, on Hutchins' Map in the account of Bouquet's Expedition in 1764; on Evans' Map of 1755 a Wyandot town is placed at the foot of Sandusky bay on the south side; this it is very probable was "Sunyendeand."*

Eighty rood—*A rod is sixteen and one-half feet, or slightly over five meters. Therefore, the town was a quarter of a mile —about three city blocks —from the mouth of the creek.*

a Dutchman.* Do you not know that when strangers come to our camp, we ought always to give them the best that we have. I acknowledged that I was wrong. He said that he could excuse this, as I was but young; but I must learn to behave like a warrior, and do great things, and never be found in any such little actions.

The lake being again calm,** we proceeded, and arrived safe at Sunyendeand, which was a Wiandot town, that lay upon a small creek which empties into the Little Lake below the mouth of Sandusky.

The town was about eighty rood above the mouth of the creek, on the south side of a large plain, on which timber grew, and nothing more but grass or nettles. In some places there were large flats, where nothing but grass grew, about three feet high when grown, and in other places nothing but nettles, very rank, where the soil was extremely rich and loose—here they planted corn. In this town there were also French traders, who purchased our skins and fur, and we all got new clothes, paint, tobacco, &c.

After I had got my new clothes, and my head done off like a red-headed wood-pecker, I, in company with a number of young Indians, went down to the

---

* The Dutch he called Skoharehaugo, which took its derivation from a Dutch settlement called Skoharey.

**The lake when calm, appears to be of a sky blue colour; though when lifted in a vessel, it is like other clear water.

corn-field, to see the squaws at work.
When we came there, they asked me to
take a hoe, which I did, and hoed for
some time. The squaws applauded me as
a good hand at the business; but when
I returned to the town, the old men
hearing of what I had done, chid me, and
said that I was adopted in the place of a
great man, and must not hoe corn like a
squaw. They never had occasion to
reprove me for any thing like this again;
as I never was extremely fond of work,
I readily complied with their orders.

As the Indians on their return from
their winter hunt, bring in with them large
quantities of bears oil, sugar, dried
venison, &c. at this time they have
plenty, and do not spare eating or giving—
thus they make way with their provision
as quick as possible. They have no such
thing as regular meals, breakfast, dinner
or supper; but if any one, even the
town folks, would go to the same house,
several times in one day, he would be
invited to eat of the best—and with
them it is bad manners to refuse to eat
when it is offered. If they will not eat it
is interpreted as a symptom of
displeasure, or that the persons refusing
to eat, were angry with those who
invited them.

At this time homony plentifully mixed
with bears' oil and sugar; or dried
venison, bears oil and sugar, is what they
offer to every one who comes in any
time of the day; and so they go on until
their sugar, bears oil and venison is
all gone, and then they have to eat
homony by itself, without bread, salt, or

any thing else; yet, still they invite every
one that comes in, to eat whilst they have
any thing to give. It is thought a shame,
not to invite people to eat, while they
have any thing; but, if they can in truth,
only say we have got nothing to eat, this
is accepted as an honorable apology. All
the hunters and warriors continued in
town about six weeks after we came in:
they spent this time in painting, going
from house to house, eating, smoking,
and playing at a game resembling dice,
or hustle-cap. They put a number of
plumb-stones in a small bowl; one side
of each stone is black, and the other
white; they then shake or hustle the bowl,
calling, hits, hits, hits, honesey, honesey,
rago, rago; which signifies calling for
white or black, or what they wish to turn
up; they then turn the bowl, and count
the whites and blacks. Some were
beating their kind of drum, and singing;
others were employed in playing on a
sort of flute, made of hollow cane; and
others playing on the jews-harp. Some
part of this time was also taken up in
attending the council house, where the
chiefs, and as many others as chose,
attended; and at night they were
frequently employed in singing and
dancing. Towards the last of this time,
which was in June 1756, they were all
engaged in preparing to go to war
against the frontiers of Virginia: when
they were equipped, they went through
their ceremonies, sung their war songs,
&c. They all marched off, from fifteen to
sixty years of age; and some boys, only
twelve years old, were equipped with

their bows and arrows, and went to war;
so that none were left in town but squaws
and children, except myself, one very
old man, and another, about fifty years
of age, who was lame.

The Indians were then in great hopes
that they would drive all the Virginians
over the lake, which is all the name they
know for the sea. They had some cause
for this hope, because, at this time,
the Americans were altogether
unacquainted with war of any kind, and
consequently very unfit to stand their
hand with such subtil enemies as the
Indians were. The two old Indians asked
me if I did not think that the Indians and
French would subdue all America, except
New-England, which they said they
had tried in old times. I told them, I
thought not: they said they had already
drove them all out of the mountains, and
had chiefly laid waste the great valley,
betwixt the North and South mountain,
from Potomack to James River, which is
a considerable part of the best land in
Virginia, Maryland, and Pennsylvania,
and that the white people appeared to
them like fools; they could neither guard
against surprize, run or fight. These, they
said, were their reasons for saying that
they would subdue the whites. They
asked me to offer my reasons for my
opinion, and told me to speak my mind
freely. I told them that the white people
to the East were very numerous, like the
trees, and though they appeared to them
to be fools, as they were not acquainted
with their way of war, yet they were not
fools; therefore, after some time they will

learn your mode of war, and turn upon you, or least defend themselves. I found that the old men themselves did not believe they could conquer America, yet they were willing to propagate the idea, in order to encourage the young men to go to war.

When the warriors left this town, we had neither meat sugar or bears oil, left. All that we had then to live on was corn pounded into coarse meal or small homony—this they boiled in water, which appeared like well thickened soup, without salt or any thing else. For some time we had plenty of this kind of homony; at length we were brought to very short allowance, and as the warriors did not return as soon as they expected, we were in a starving condition, and but one gun in the town, and very little ammunition. The old lame Wiandot concluded that he would go a hunting in a canoe, and take me with him, and try to kill deer in the water, as it was then watering time. We went up Sandusky a few miles, then turned up a creek, and encamped. We had lights prepared, as we were to hunt in the night, and also a piece of bark and some bushes set up in the canoe, in order to conceal ourselves from the deer. A little boy that was with us, held the light, I worked the canoe, and the old man, who had his gun loaded with large shot, when we came near the deer, fired, and in this manner killed three deer, in part of one night. We went to our fire, ate heartily, and in the morning returned to town, in order to relieve the hungry and distressed.

Hunt in the night—The method of night hunting deer which Smith describes was a very effective one. The light of the candle or torch attracted curious deer and reflected in their eyes, making a good target for the hunter. While the body of the animal would fade into the background, its eyes would shine like two lamps. John Brickell and Jonathan Alder both learned this method of hunting while captive among the Ohio Indians.

When we came to town, the children were crying bitterly on account of pinching hunger. We delivered what we had taken, and though it was but little among so many, it was divided according to the strictest rules of justice. We immediately set out for another hunt, but before we returned a part of the warriors had come in, and brought with them on horse-back, a quantity of meat. These warriors had divided into different parties, and all struck at different places in Augusta county. They brought in with them a considerable number of scalps, prisoners, horses, and other plunder. One of the parties brought in with them, one Arthur Campbell, that is now Col. Campbell, who lives on Holston River, near the Royal-Oak. As the Wiandots at Sunyendeand, and those at Detroit were connected, Mr. Campbell was taken to Detroit; but he remained some time with me in this town: his company was very agreeable, and I was sorry when he left me. During his stay at Sunyendeand he borrowed my Bible, and made some pertinent remarks on what he had read. One passage was where it is said, "It is good for man that he bear the yoke in his youth." He said we ought to be resigned to the will of Provikence, as we were now bearing the yoke, in our youth. Mr. Campbell appeared to be then about sixteen or seventeen years of age.

There was a number of prisoners brought in by these parties, and when they were to run the gauntlet, I went and told them how they were to act. One John Savage, was brought in, a middle

Augusta County — This county is located in the northwestern section of Virginia.

Arthur Campbell—*Colonel Arthur Campbell of Washington county in Southwestern Virginia. He escaped from the Indians about three years after meeting with Smith, and returned by way of Fort Pitt to Virginia, where he afterward became distinguished in civil and military life, particularly as commander in a successful expedition against the Cherokees in 1781. He was a delegate from Fincastle county to the Virginia Revolutionary Convention of 1776. The Royal Oak ford of the Holston river is in the present county of Smythe about three miles east of the town of Marion. Colonel Campbell removed to Knox county, Kentucky, where he died in 1816 in the 74th year of his age.*

aged man, or about forty years old. He was to run the gauntlet. I told him what he had to do; and after this I fell into one of the ranks with the Indians, shouting and yelling like them; and as they were not very severe on him, as he passed me, I hit him with a piece of pumpkin—which pleased the Indians much, but hurt my feelings.

About the time that these warriors came in, the green corn was beginning to be of use; so that we had either green corn or venison, and sometimes both— which was comparatively, high living. When we could have plenty of green corn, or roasting-ears, the hunters became lazy, and spent their time as already mentioned, in singing and dancing &c. They appeared to be fulfilling the scriptures beyond those who profess to believe them, in that of taking no thought of to-morrow: and also in living in love, peace and friendship together, without disputes. In this respect, they shame those who profess Christianity.

In this manner we lived, until October, then the geese, swans, ducks, cranes, &c. came from the north, and alighted on this little Lake, without number or innumerable. Sunyendeand is a remarkable place for fish, in the spring, and fowl both in the fall and spring.

As our hunters were now tired with indolence, and fond of their own kind of exercise, they all turned out to fowling, and in this could scarce miss of success; so that we had now plenty of homony and the best of fowls; and sometimes as a rarity we had a little bread, which

Little Lake—*Sandusky bay. It is about twenty miles long and from one to four miles wide. It was formerly "termed by the inhabitants the Little Lake."* . . .

*Sa-undustee*, water, in the Wyandot tongue. . . . *By changing the pronunciation the meaning of this and other words in the Wyandot language, expressing proper names, varied.* Sah-un-dus-kee, *clear water.* Sa-anduste, *or water within water pools.* . . . *The latter signification is peculiarly applicable to Sandusky bay and the extensive marshes on its borders, which are inter-sected in many directions by pools and channels of open water.*

was made of Indian corn meal, pounded
in a homony-block, mixed with boiled
beans, and baked in cakes under the ashes.

This, with us was called good living,
though not equal to our fat, roasted and
boiled venison, when we went to the
woods in the fall; or bears meat and
beaver in the winter; or sugar, bears oil,
and dry venison in the spring.

Some time in October, another
adopted brother, older than Tontileaugo,
came to pay us a visit at Sunyendeand,
and he asked me to take a hunt with
him on Cayahaga. As they always used
me as a free man, and gave me the liberty
of choosing, I told him that I was attached
to Tontileaugo—had never seen him
before, and therefore, asked sometime
to consider of this. He told me that the
party he was going with would not be
along, or at the mouth of this little lake,
in less than six days, and I could in this
time be acquainted with him, and judge
for myself. I consulted with Tontileaugo
on this occasion, and he told me that
our old brother Tecaughretanego,
(which was his name) was a chief, and a
better man that he was; and if I went
with him I might expect to be well used,
but he said I might do as I pleased;
and if I staid he would use me as he had
done. I told him that he had acted in
every respect as a brother to me; yet I
was much pleased with my old brother's
conduct and conversation; and as he was
going to a part of the country I had never
been in, I wished to go with him—he said
that he was perfectly willing.

I then went with Tecaughretanego,

The Caghnawagas—*An ancient tribe of the Mohawks in the interest of the French, who early in the last century induced them to remove from New York, and settle at the rapids of St. Louis near Montreal. . . . [They are also] called the Praying Indians.*

Many of the Caughnawagas, or French Mohawks, moved into the Sandusky and Scioto river areas in Ohio during the French and Indian War period.

In the years after the American Revolution and on into the nineteenth century, numbers of these Caughnawagas served the fur trade as hunters and trappers in the far west. They were commonly known as Iroquois, as the Mohawks were part of the Iroquois Confederacy.

Flags—These were most likely rushes or cattails.

to the mouth of the little lake, where he met with the company he intended going with, which was composed of Caughnewagas, and Ottawas.—Here I was introduced to a Caughnewaga sister, and others I had never before seen. My sister's name was Mary, which they pronounced Maully. I asked Tecaughretanego how it came that she had an English name; he said that he did not know that it was an English name; but it was the name the priest gave her when she was baptized, which he said was the name of the mother of Jesus. He said there were a great many of the Caughnewagas and Wiandots that were a kind of half Roman-Catholics; but as for himself, he said, that the priest and him could not agree; as they held notions that contradicted both sense and reason, and had the assurance to tell him, that the book of God, taught them these foolish absurdities: but he could not believe the great and good spirit ever taugh them any such nonsense: and therefore he concluded that the Indians' old religion was better than this new way of worshiping God.

The Ottawas have a very useful kind of tents which they carry with them, made of flags, plaited and stitched together in a very artful manner, so as to turn rain, or wind well,—each mat is made fifteen feet long, and about five feet broad. In order to erect this kind of tent, they cut a number of long strait poles, which they drive in the ground, in form of a circle, leaning inwards; then they spread the matts

on these poles,—beginning at the
bottom and extending up, leaving only
a hole in the top uncovered—and this
hole answers the place of a chimney.
They make a fire of dry split wood, in
the middle, and spread down bark mats
and skins for bedding, on which they
sleep in a crooked posture, all round the
fire, as the length of their beds will not
admit of stretching themselves. In place
of a door they lift up one end of a mat
and creep in, and let the mat fall down
behind them.

These tents are warm and dry, and
tolerable clear of smoke. Their lumber
they keep under birch-bark canoes,
which they carry out and turn up for a
shelter, where they keep every thing
from the rain. Nothing is in the tents
but themselves and their bedding.

This company had four birch canoes and
four tents. We were kindly received, and
they gave us plenty of homony, and wild
fowl, boiled and roasted. As the geese,
ducks, swans, &c. here are well grain-fed,
they were remarkably fat, especially
the green necked ducks.

The wild fowl here, feed upon a kind of
wild rice, that grows spontaneously
in the shallow water, or wet places
along the sides or in the corners of the
lakes.

As the wind was high and we could not
proceed on our voyage, we remained here
several days, and killed abundance of wild
fowl, and a number of racoons.

When a company of Indians are
moving together on the lake, as it is at
this time of the year often dangerous

Tent—The conical shelter Smith describes here, a framework of poles covered with flag or cattail mats, also was used by other Woodland Indians. This form of the tepee was useful to hunting parties or other groups on the move who required a temporary shelter. The covering might also be birch, elm, or some other type of bark.

The Plains Indians of the west developed the tepee into a fine type of portable shelter or tent with a cover of buffalo hide. The western tepees were usually larger than those Smith describes.

Wild rice—Really a grass (*Zizania aquatica*), wild rice was an important supplement to wild game in the Indian diet. It grew abundantly in the northern lake country and still does. The Indians harvested rice in large quantities in September. Like maple sugar, wild rice was sold or bartered to the traders.

sailing, the old men hold a council; and when they agree to embark, every one is engaged immediately in making ready, without offering one word against the measure, though the lake may be boisterous and horrid. One morning tho' the wind appeared to me to be as high as in days past, and the billows raging, yet the call was given yohoh-yohoh, which was quickly answered by all— ooh-ooh which signifies agreed. We were all instantly engaged in preparing to start, and had considerable difficulties in embarking.

As soon as we got into our canoes we fell to paddling with all our might, making out from the shore. Though these sort of canoes ride waves beyond what could be expected, yet the water several times dashed into them. When we got out about half a mile from shore, we hoisted sail, and as it was nearly a west wind, we then seemed to ride the waves with ease, and went on at a rapid rate. We then all laid down our paddles, excepting one that steered, and there was no water dashed into our canoes, until we came near the shore again. We sailed about sixty miles that day, and encamped some time before night.

The next day we again embarked and went on very well for some time; but the lake being boisterous, and the wind not fair, we were obliged to make to shore, which we accomplished with hard work and some difficulty in landing.—The next morning a council was held by the old men.

As we had this day to pass by a long

precipice of rocks, on the shore about
nine miles, which rendered it impossible
for us to land, though the wind was high
and the lake rough; yet, as it was fair,
we were all ordered to embark. We
wrought ourselves out from the shore
and hoisted sail (what we used in place
of sail cloth, were our tent mats, which
answered the place very well) and went
on for some time with a fair wind, until
we were opposite to the precipice, and
then it turned towards the shore, and we
began to fear we should be cast upon
the rocks. Two of the canoes were
considerably farther out from the rocks,
than the canoe I was in. Those who were
farthest out in the lake did not let down
their sails until they had passed the
precipice; but as we were nearer the
rock, we were obliged to lower our sails,
and paddle with all our might. With
much difficulty we cleared ourselves of
the rock, and landed. As the other canoes
had landed before us, there were
immediately runners sent off to see if
we were all safely landed.

This night the wind fell, and the next
morning the lake was tolerably calm, and
we embarked without difficulty, and
paddled along near the shore, until we
came to the mouth of Cayahaga, which
empties into Lake Erie on the south side,
betwixt Canesadooharie and Presq'
Isle.

We turned up Cayahaga and encamped
—where we staid and hunted for several
days; and so we kept moving and hunting
until we came to the forks of Cayahaga.

This is a very gentle river, and but few

Cuyahoga — Ka-ih-ogh-ha.
River, in the Mohawk tongue.

Presq' Isle—Presque Isle
is located at Erie, Penn-
sylvania.

Rapids—*The falls of the Cuyahoga river in Summit county four miles north-east of Akron. The descent is about 200 feet in 2 1/2 miles.*

Carrying place—*The old Indian Portage Path between the Tuscarawas branch of the Muskingum river, and the Cuyahoga, in Portage and Coventry townships in the present county of Summit. It was about eight miles in length. On the Maps of Evans and Hutchins it is laid down "1 mile Portage."*

We buried our canoes—Smith mentions several times in his narrative that the Indian canoes were buried for winter storage. It was a simple way to protect them from the elements and kept the bark from drying out.

It is probable that dugout canoes were also buried or weighted with stones and kept under water when not in use for a considerable length of time.

riffles, or swift running places, from the mouth to the forks. Deer here were tolerably plenty, large and fat; but bear and other game scarce. The upland is hilly, and principally second and third rate land. The timber chiefly black-oak, white-oak, hickory, dogwood &c. The bottoms are rich and large, and the timber is walnut, locust, mulberry, sugar-tree, red-haw, black-haw, wild-appletrees &c. The West Branch of this river interlocks with the East Branch of Muskingum; and the East Branch with the Big Beaver creek, that empties into the Ohio about thirty miles below Pittsburgh.

From the forks of Cayahaga to the East Branch of Muskingum, there is a carrying place, where the Indians carry their canoes &c. from the waters of Lake Erie, into the waters of the Ohio.

From the forks I went over with some hunters, to the East Branch of Muskingum, where they killed several deer, a number of beavers, and returned heavy laden, with skins and meat, which we carried on our backs, as we had no horses.

The land here is chiefly second and third rate, and the timber chiefly oak and hickory. A little above the forks, on the East Branch of Cayahaga, are considerable rapids, very rocky for some distance; but no perpendicular falls.

About the first of December, 1756, we were preparing for leaving the river: we buried our canoes, and as usual hung up our skins, and every one had a pack to carry: the squaws also packed up their tents, which they carried in large rolls, that extended up above their heads;

and though a great bulk, yet not heavy.
We steered about a south east course,
and could not march over ten miles per
day. At night we lodged in our flag tents,
which when erected, were nearly in the
shape of a sugar loaf, and about fifteen
feet diameter at the ground.

In this manner we proceeded about
forty miles, and wintered in these tents,
on the waters of Beaver creek, near a little
lake or large pond, which is about two
miles long, and one broad, and a
remarkable place for beaver.

It is a received opinion among the
Indians, that the geese turn to beavers,
and the snakes to racoons; and though
Tecaughretanego, who was a wise man,
was not fully persuaded that this was
true; yet he seemed in some measure to
be carried away with this whimsical
notion. He said that this pond had been
always a great place of beaver. Though
he said he knew them to be frequently all
killed, (as he thought;) yet the next
winter they would be as plenty as ever.
And as the beaver was an animal that
did not travel by land, and there being no
water communication, to, or from this
pond—how could such a number of
beavers get there year after year? But as
this pond was also a considerable place
for geese, when they came in the fall
from the north, and alighted in this pond,
they turned beavers, all but the feet,
which remained nearly the same.

I said, that though there was no water
communication, in, or out of this pond; yet
it appeared that it was fed by springs, as
it was always clear and never stagnated:

Flag tents—These were
similar to the modern
canvas-covered tepee,
about twelve to fourteen
feet in diameter, which
will accommodate three
adults comfortably for
sleeping and camping.
The great advantage of
a tepee this size is that
in cold weather a small
fire built in the center
will keep the occupants
warm.

Little Lake—*One of the
numerous Beaver Ponds on the
head waters of the Mahon-
ing—no doubt much dimin-
ished in extent since the clear-
ing of the forest, and the
drainage of the land. It may
be found however in the
southern part of Mahoning
county.*

and as a very large spring rose about a
mile below this pond, it was likely that
this spring came from this pond. In the
fall, when this spring is comparatively low,
there would be air under ground sufficient
for the beavers to breathe in, with their
heads above water, for they cannot live
long under water, and so they might have
a subterraneous passage by water into
this pond.—Tecaughretanego, granted
that it might be so.

About the sides of this pond there grew
great abundance of cranberries, which
the Indians gathered up on the ice, when
the pond was frozen over. These berries
were about as large as rifle bullets—of a
bright red color—an agreeable sour,
though rather too sour of themselves; but
when mixed with sugar, had a very
agreeable taste.

In conversation with Tecaughretanego,
I happened to be talking of the beavers'
catching fish. He asked me why I
thought that the beaver caught fish? I
told him that I had read of the beaver
making dams for the conveniency of
fishing. He laughed, and made game of
me and my book. He said the man that
wrote that book knew nothing about
the beaver. The beaver never did eat
flesh of any kind; but lived on the bark
of trees, roots, and other vegetables.

In order to know certainly how this was,
when we killed a beaver I carefully
examined the intestines but found no
appearance of fish; I afterwards made
an experiment on a pet beaver which we
had, and found that it would neither eat
fish or flesh; therefore I acknowledged

that the book I had read was wrong.

I asked him if the beaver was an amphibious animal, or if it could live under water? He said that the beaver was a kind of subterraneous water animal, that lives in or near the water; but they were no more amphibious than the ducks and geese were—which was constantly proven to be the case; as all the beavers that are caught in steel traps are drowned, provided the trap be heavy enough to keep them under water. As the beaver does not eat fish, I inquired of Tecaughretanego why the beaver made such large dams? He said they were of use to them in various respects—both for their safety and food. For their safety, as by raising the water over the mouths of their holes, or subterraneous lodging places, they could not be easily found: and as the beaver feeds chiefly on the bark of trees, by raising the water over the banks, they can cut down saplings for bark to feed upon without going out much upon the land: and when they are obliged to go out on land for this food they frequently are caught by the wolves. As the beaver can run upon land, but little faster than a water tortoise, and is no fighting animal, if they are any distance from the water they become an easy prey to their enemies.

I asked Tecaughretanego, what was the use of the beaver's stones, or glands, to them;—as the she beaver has two pair, which is commonly called the oil stones, and the bark stones? He said that as the beavers are the dumbest of all animals, and scarcely ever make any noise; and as they were working creatures, they made use of this smell in order to work in concert. If an old beaver was to come on the bank and rub his breech upon the ground, and raise a perfume, the others will collect from different places and go to work: this is also of use to them in travelling, that they may thereby search out and find their company. Cunning hunters finding this out, have made use of it against the beavers, in order to catch them. What is the bait which you see them make use of, but a compound of the oil and bark stones? By this perfume, which is only a false signal they decoy them to the trap.

Near this pond, beaver was the principal game. Before the waters froze up, we caught a great many with wooden and steel traps: but after that, we hunted the beaver on the ice. Some places here the beavers build large houses to live in; and in other places they have subterraneous lodgings in the banks. Where they lodge in the ground we have no chance of hunting them on the ice; but where they have houses we go with malls and handspikes, and break all the hollow ice, to prevent them from getting their heads above the water under it. Then we break a hole in the house, and they make their escape into the water; but as they cannot live long under water, they are obliged to go to some of those broken places to breathe, and the Indians commonly put in their hands, catch them by the hind leg, hawl them on the ice, and tomahawk them. Sometimes they shoot them in the head, when they raise

Wooden and steel traps —Wooden "deadfalls" constructed of logs and saplings, and funnel traps made of poles were used by Indian beaver hunters. These devices were designed to crush or drown the beaver when trapped. Nets were also used; when netted, the beaver was hauled out and clubbed to death.

Hand-forged steel traps were obtained by the Indians from the traders. These were leg-hold traps and were set in such a way that the beaver was drowned when caught.

it above the water. I asked the Indians
if they were not afraid to catch the beavers
with their hands? they said no: they
were not much of a biting creature; yet
if they would catch them by the fore foot
they would bite.

I went out with Tecaughretanego,
and some others a beaver hunting: but we
did not succeed, and on our return we
saw where several racoons had passed,
while the snow was soft; tho' there was
now a crust upon it, we all made a halt
looking at the racoon tracks. As they
saw a tree with a hole in it they told me
to go and see if they had gone in thereat;
and if they had to halloo, and they would
come and take them out. When I went to
that tree, I found they had gone past;
but I saw another the way they had
went, and proceeded to examine that,
and found they had gone up it. I then
began to holloo, but could have no
answer.

As it began to snow and blow most
violently, I returned and proceeded after
my company, and for some time could
see their tracks; but the old snow being
only about three inches deep, and a
crust upon it, the present driving snow
soon filled up the tracks. As I had only
a bow, arrows and tomahawk, with me,
and no way to strike fire, I appeared to be
in a dismal situation—and as the air was
dark with snow, I had little more prospect
of steering my course, than I would in
the night. At length I came to a hollow
tree, with a hole at one side that I
could go in at. I went in, and found that
it was a dry place, and the hollow about

All the clothes I had—While Indians seem to have been able to withstand cold weather better than white men, Smith is obviously not clothed for cold weather. Some of the Indians' clothing especially made for winter included: moccasins stuffed with dry moss or lined with hair or fur; blankets woven from strips of rabbit pelts or tanned buffalo or beaver pelt robes; and capote coats, a type of overcoat probably of French-Canadian origin, made from trade blankets.

three feet diameter, and high enough for me to stand in. I found that there was also a considerable quantity of soft, dry rotten wood, around this hollow: I therefore concluded that I would lodge here; and that I would go to work, and stop up the door of my house. I stripped off my blanket, (which was all the clothes that I had, excepting a breech-clout, leggins and mockasons,) and with my tomahawk, fell to chopping at the top of a fallen tree that lay near and carried wood and set it up on end against the door, until I had it three or four feet thick, all round, excepting a hole I had left to creep in at. I had a block prepared that I could hawl after me, to stop this hole: and before I went in I put in a number of small sticks, that I might more effectually stop it on the inside. When I went in, I took my tomahawk and cut down all the dry rotten wood I could get, and beat it small. With it I made a bed like a goose-nest or hog-bed, and with the small sticks stopped every hole, until my house was almost dark. I stripped off my mockasons, and danced in the centre of my bed for about half an hour, in order to warm myself. In this time my feet and whole body were agreeably warmed. The snow, in the mean while, had stopped all the holes, so that my house was as dark as a dungeon; though I knew it could not yet be dark out of doors. I then coiled myself up in my blanket, lay down in my little round bed, and had a tolerable nights lodging. When I awoke, all was dark—not the least glimmering of light was to be seen.

Immediately I recollected that I was not
to expect light in this new habitation,
as there was neither door nor window in
it. As I could hear the storm raging, and
did not suffer much cold, as I was then
situated, I concluded I would stay in my
nest until I was certain it was day. When
I had reason to conclude that it surely was
day, I arose and put on my mockasons,
which I had laid under my head to keep
from Freezing. I then endeavored to find
the door, and had to do all by the sense
of feeling, which took me some time.
At length I found the block, but it being
heavy, and a large quantity of snow
having fallen on it, at the first attempt I
did not move it. I then felt terrified—
among all the hardships I had sustained,
I never knew before, what it was to be
thus deprived of light. This, with the
other circumstances attending it,
appeared grievous. I went straightway
to bed again, wrapped my blanket
round me, and lay and mused awhile,
and then prayed to Almighty God to
direct and protect me, as he had done
heretofore. I once again attempted to
move away the block, which proved
successful: it moved about nine inches—
With this a considerable quantity of
snow fell in from above, and I immediately
received light; so that I found a very great
snow had fallen, above what I had ever
seen in one night. I then knew why I
could not easily move the block, and I
was so rejoiced at obtaining the light,
that all my other difficulties seemed to
vanish. I then turned into my cell, and
returned God thanks for having once more

received the light of Heaven. At length I belted my blanket about me, got my tomahawk, bow and arrows, and went out of my den.

I was now in tolerable high spirits, tho' the snow had fallen above three feet deep, in addition to what was on the ground before; and the only imperfect guide I had, in order to steer my course to camp, was the trees; as the moss generally grows on the north-west side of them, if they are straight. I proceeded on, wading through the snow, and about twelve o'clock (as it appeared afterwards, from that time to night, for it was yet cloudy,) I came upon the creek that our camp was on, about half a mile below the camp; and when I came in sight of the camp, I found that there was great joy, by the shouts and yelling of the boys, &c.

When I arrived, they all came round me, and received me gladly; but at this time no questions were asked, and I was taken into a tent, where they gave me plenty of fat beaver meat, and then asked me to smoke. When I had done, Tecaughretanego desired me to walk out to a fire they had made. I went out, and they all collected round me, both men women and boys. Tecaughretanego asked me to give them a particular account of what had happened from the time they left me yesterday, until now. I told them the whole of the story, and they never interrupted me; but when I made a stop, the intervals were filled with loud acclamations of joy. As I could not, at this time, talk Ottawa or Jibewa well,

Jibewa—The Ojibway, also known as Chippewa, were a numerous Algonquian people who occupied a large territory around Lake Huron and Lake Superior.

(which is nearly the same) I delivered
my story in Caughnewaga. As my sister
Molly's husband was a Jibewa and
could understand Caughnewaga, he acted
as interpreter, and delivered my story to
the Jibewas and Ottawas, which they
received with pleasure. When all this was
done, Tecaughretanego made a speech
to me in the following manner:

   "Brother,

   "You see we have prepared snow-shoes
to go after you, and were almost ready
to go, when you appeared; yet, as you had
not been accustomed to hardships in
your country, to the east, we never
expected to see you alive. Now, we are
glad to see you in various respects: we
are glad to see you on your own account;
and we are glad to see the prospect of
your filling the place of a great man, in
whose room you were adopted. We do
not blame you for what has happened,
we blame ourselves; because, we did not
think of this driving snow filling up the
tracks, until after we came to camp.

   "Brother,

   "Your conduct on this occasion hath
pleased us much: you have given us an
evidence of your fortitude, skill and
resolution: and we hope you will always
go on to do great actions, as it is only
great actions that can make a great man."

   I told my brother Tecaughretanego,
that I thanked them for their care of me,
and for the kindness I always received.
I told him that I always wished to do
great actions, and hoped I never would
do any thing to dishonor any of those with
whom I was connected. I likewise told

my Jibewa brother-in-law to tell his people that I also thanked them for their care and kindness.

The next morning some of the hunters went out on snow-shoes, killed several deer, and hauled some of them into camp upon the snow. They fixed their carrying strings, (which are broad in the middle, and small at each end,) in the fore feet and nose of the deer, and laid the broad part of it on their heads or about their shoulders, and pulled it along; and when it is moving, will not sink in the snow much deeper than a snow-shoe; and when taken with the grain of the hair, slips along very easy.

The snow-shoes are made like a hoop-net, and wrought with buck-skin thongs. Each shoe is about two feet and a half long, and about eighteen inches broad, before, and small behind, with cross bars, in order to fix or tie them to their feet. After the snow had lay a few days, the Indians tomahawked the deer, by pursuing them in this manner.

About two weeks after this there came a warm rain, and took away the chief part of the snow, and broke up the ice: then we engaged in making wooden traps to catch beavers, as we had but few steel traps. These traps are made nearly in the same manner as the racoon traps already described.

One day as I was looking after my traps, I got benighted, by beaver ponds intercepting my way to camp; and as I had neglected to take fire-works with me, and the weather very cold, I could find no suitable lodging place, therefore the

Fire-works — Smith is referring to the common fire-strikers of pioneer times—when flint was struck against steel, the resulting sparks ignited punk or charred rags. These sparks were nursed into embers used to light a fire.

A flintlock gun or rifle could also have been used as its ignition system created a shower of sparks when the flint struck the steel frizzen of the lock.

only expedient I could think of to keep
myself from freezing, was exercise. I
danced and hallo'd the whole night with
all my might, and the next day came to
camp. Though I suffered much more this
time than the other night I lay out, yet the
Indians were not so much concerned,
as they thought I had fire works with me;
but when they knew how it was, they did
not blame me. They said that old hunters
were frequently involved in this place,
as the beaver dams were one above
another on every creek and run, so that
it is hard to find a fording place. They
applauded me for my fortitude, and said,
as they had now plenty of beaver-skins,
they would purchase me a new gun at
Detroit, as we were to go there the next
spring; and then if I should chance to be
lost in dark weather, I could make fire,
kill provision, and return to camp when
the sun shined. By being bewildered on
the waters of Muskingum, I lost repute,
and was reduced to the bow and arrow;
and by lying out two nights here, I regained
my credit.

   After some time the waters all froze
again, and then, as formerly, we hunted
beavers on the ice. Though beaver meat,
without salt or bread, was the chief of our
food this winter, yet we had always
plenty, and I was well contented with
my diet, as it appeared delicious fare, after
the way we had lived the winter before.

   Sometime in February, we scaffolded up
our fur and skins, and moved about ten
miles in quest of a sugar camp, or a
suitable place to make sugar, and
encamped in a large bottom, on the head

waters of Big Beaver creek. We had
some difficulty in moving, as we had a
blind Caughnewaga boy, about fifteen
years of age, to lead; and as this country
is very brushy we frequently had him to
carry;—We had also my Jibewa brother-
in-law's father with us, who was thought
by the Indians to be a great conjuror
—his name was Manetohcoa—this old
man was so decrepit, that we had to carry
him this route upon a bier,—and all our
baggage to pack on our backs.

Shortly after we came to this place the
squaws began to make sugar. We had no
large kettles with us this year, and they
made the frost, in some measure, supply
the place of fire, in making sugar. Their
large bark vessels, for holding the stock-
water, they made broad and shallow; and
as the weather is very cold here, it
frequently freezes at night in sugar
time; and the ice they break and cast out
of the vessels. I asked them if they were
not throwing away the sugar? they said,
no: it was water they were casting away,
sugar did not freeze, and there was
scarcely any in that ice. They said I might
try the experiment, and boil some of it,
and see what I would get. I never did
try it; but I observed that after several
times freezing, the water that remained
in the vessel, changed its color and
became brown and very sweet.

About the time we were done making
sugar the snow went off the ground; and
one night a squaw raised an alarm. She
said she saw two men with guns in their
hands, upon the bank on the other side of
the creek, spying our tents—they were

supposed to be Johnston's Mohawks. On this the squaws were ordered to slip quietly out, some distance into the bushes; and all who had either guns or bows were to squat in the bushes near the tents; and if the enemy rushed up, we were to give them the first fire, and let the squaws have an opportunity of escaping. I got down beside Tecaughretanego, and he whispered to me not to be afraid, for he would speak to the Mohawks, and as they spoke the same tongue that we did, they would not hurt the Caughnewagas, or me: but they would kill all the Jibewas and Ottawas that they could, and take us along with them. This news pleased me well, and I heartily wished for the approach of the Mohawks.

Before we withdrew from the tents they had carried Manetohcoa to the fire, and gave him his conjuring tools; which were dyed feathers, the bone of the shoulder blade of a wild cat, tobacco &c. and while we were in the bushes, Manetohcoa was in a tent at the fire, conjuring away to the utmost of his ability. At length he called aloud for us all to come in, which was quickly obeyed. When we came in, he told us that after he had gone through the whole of his ceremony, and expected to see a number of Mohawks on the flat bone when it was warmed at the fire, the pictures of two wolves only appeared. He said, tho there were no Mohawks about, we must not be angry with the squaw for giving a false alarm; as she had occasion to go out and happened to see the wolves,

Johnson's Mohawks—*Sir William Johnson, Superintendent of the affairs of the Six Nations, and other Northern Indians. The Mohawks adopted him as a member of their nation, with the rank of war chief, in 1746. He resided near the Mohawk villages at Johnstown, now in Fulton county, New York.*

Conjuring tools — The tools or objects used by a conjuror might be anything to which the magician attached occult power: animal teeth or bones, an odd stone, some object with an unusual origin, or anything secured under circumstances that suggested magic.

An Indian conjuror was considered a magician and sometimes a medical doctor who was brought in to attend sick or injured persons. The Moravian missionaries had little respect for the conjurors, and considered them to be clever tricksters. However, the missionaries did recognize the true skills and knowledge of Indian medical doctors, men who had considerable success in healing wounds, broken bones, and curing some diseases.

thought it was moon light, yet she got afraid, and she conceited it was Indians, with guns in their hands, so he said we might all go to sleep for there was no danger—and accordingly we did.

The next morning we went to the place, and found wolf tracks, and where they had scratched with their feet like dogs; but there was no sign of mockason tracks. If there is any such thing as a wizzard, I think Manetohcoa was as likely to be one, as any man, as he was a professed worshipper of the devil.—But let him be a conjuror or not, I am persuaded that the Indians believed what he told them upon this occasion, as well as if it had come from an infallible oracle; or they would not after such an alarm as this, go all to sleep in an unconcerned manner. This appeared to me the most like witchcraft, of any thing I beheld while I was with them. Though I scrutinized their proceedings in business of this kind, yet I generally found that their pretended witchcraft, was either art or mistaken notions whereby they deceived themselves.—Before a battle they spy the enemy's motions carefully, and when they find that they can have considerable advantage, and the greatest prospect of success, then the old men pretend to conjure, or to tell what the event will be, —and this they do in a figurative manner, which will bear something of a different interpretation, which generally comes to pass nearly as they foretold; therefore the young warriors generally believed these old conjurors, which had a tendency to animate, and excite them to push on with vigor.

Some time in March 1757 we began to
move back to the forks of Cayahaga,
which was about forty or fifty miles; and
as we had no horses, we had all our
baggage and several hundred weight of
beaver skins, and some deer and bear
skins all to pack on our backs. The method
we took to accomplish this, was by
making short day's journies. In the
morning we would move on with as much
as we were able to carry, about five
miles, and encamp; and then run back for
more. We commonly made three such
trips in the day. When we came to the
great pond, we staid there one day to rest
ourselves and to kill ducks and geese.

While we remained here, I went in
company with a young Caughnewaga,
who was about sixteen or seventeen years
of age, Chinnohete by name, in order to
gather crannberries. As he was gathering
berries at some distance from me, three
Jibewa squaws crept up undiscovered,
and made at him speedily, but he nimbly
escaped, and came to me apparently
terrified. I asked him what he was afraid
of? he replied, did you not see those
squaws? I told him I did, and they
appeared to be in a very good humour.
I asked him, wherefore then he was afraid
of them? He said the Jibewa squaws
were very bad women, and had a very
ugly custom among them. I asked him
what that custom was? he said, that when
two or three of them could catch a young
lad, that was betwixt a man and a boy,
out by himself, if they could overpower
him, they would strip him by force in

order to see whether he was coming on to be a man or not. He said that was what they intended when they crawled up, and ran so violently at him, but said he, I am very glad that I so narrowly escaped. I then agreed with Chinnohete in condemning this as a bad custom, and an exceedingly immodest action for young women to be guilty of.

From our sugar camp on the head waters of Big Beaver creek to this place, is not hilly, in some places the woods are tolerably clear: but in most places exceedingly brushy. The land here is chiefly second and third rate. The timber on the upland is white-oak, black-oak, hickory, and chesnut: there is also in some places walnut up land, and plenty of good water. The bottoms here are generally large and good.

We again proceeded on from the pond to the forks of Cayahaga, at the rate of about five miles per day.

The land on this route is not very hilly, it is well watered, and, in many places ill timbered, generally brushy, and chiefly second and third rate land, intermixed with good bottoms.

When we came to the forks, we found that the skins we had scaffolded were all safe. Though this was a public place, and Indians frequently passing, and our skins hanging up in view; yet there were none stolen; and it is seldom that Indians do steal any thing from one another; and they say they never did, until the white people came among them, and learned some of them, to lie, cheat, and steal,—but, be that as it may, they never

To lie, cheat, and steal— Many white men employed in the fur trade were of low character. Often they were brutal and vicious, poor representatives of their race who had a bad influence on the Indians. Not all traders were of this type, but too many were.

Christopher Gist wrote of talking with a white woman taken captive as a child in February of 1704 in the French and Indian raid on Deerfield, Massachusetts. Gist met her on January 15, 1751, at a small Indian town on White Woman's Creek in present day Coshocton County. He recorded that: "Her name is Mary Harris, she still remembers they used to be very religious in New England, and wonders how the White Men (traders), can be so wicked as she has seen them in these Woods."

did curse or swear, until the whites
learned them; some think their language
will not admit of it, but I am not of that
opinion, if I was so disposed, I could find
language to curse or swear, in the Indian
tongue.

I remember that Tecaughretanego,
when something displeased him, said,
God damn it.—I asked him if he knew what
he then said? he said he did; and
mentioned one of their degrading
expressions, which he supposed to be
the meaning or something like the
meaning of what he had said. I told him
that it did not bear the least resemblance
to it; that what he had said, was calling
upon the great spirit to punish the
object he was displeased with. He stood
for some time amazed, and then said,
if this be the meaning of these words
what sort of people are the whites? when
the traders were among us these words
seemed to be intermixed with all their
discourse. He told me to reconsider what
I had said, for he thought I must be
mistaken in my definition; if I was not
mistaken, he said, the traders applied
these words not only wickedly, but
oftentimes very foolishly and contrary to
sense or reason. He said, he remembered
once of a traders' accidentally breaking
his gun lock, and on that occasion calling
out aloud God damn it—surely said he
the gun lock was not an object worthy of
punishment for Owaneeyo, or the Great
Spirit: he also observed the traders
often used this expression when they were
in a good humour and not displeased with
any thing.—I acknowledged that the

traders used this expression very often, in a most irrational, inconsistent, and impious manner; yet I still asserted that I had given the true meaning of these words.—He replied, if so, the traders are as bad as Oonasahroona, or the under ground inhabitants, which is the name they give the devils; as they entertain a notion that their place of residence is under the earth.

We took up our birch-bark canoes which we had buried, and found that they were not damaged by the winter; but they not being sufficient to carry all that we now had, we made a large chesnut bark canoe; as elm bark was not to be found at this place.

We all embarked, and had a very agreeable passage down the Cayahaga, and along the south side of Lake Erie, until we passed the mouth of Sandusky; then the wind arose, and we put in at the mouth of the Miami of the Lake, at Cedar Point, where we remained several days, and killed a number of Turkeys, geese, ducks, and swans. The wind being fair, and the lake not extremely rough, we again embarked, hoisted up sails, and arrived safe at the Wiandot town, nearly opposite to Fort Detroit, on the north side of the river. Here we found a number of French traders, every one very willing to deal with us for our beaver.

We bought ourselves fine clothes, amunition, paint, tobacco, &c. and, according to promise, they purchased me a new gun: yet we had parted with only about one third of our beaver. At

Miami of the Lake—the Maumee River.

Fort Detroit—Founded by the French in 1701, Fort Detroit was stratigically located on the Detroit River between Lakes Huron and Erie. It was important as a military post and a fur trading center.

Following the French and Indian War, Detroit was occupied by the British in 1763 and besieged by the Indians for nearly a year during Pontiac's War. During the Revolution, Detroit was a hub for British and Indian campaigns against the American western frontier.

length a trader came to town with French Brandy: We purchased a keg of it, and held a council about who was to get drunk, and who was to keep sober. I was invited to get drunk, but I refused the proposal—then they told me that I must be one of those who were to take care of the drunken people. I did not like this; but of two evils I chose that which I thought was the least—and fell in with those who were to conceal the arms, and keep every dangerous weapon we could, out of their way, and endeavor, if possible to keep the drinking club from killing each other, which was a very hard task. Several times we hazarded our own lives, and got ourselves hurt, in preventing them from slaying each other. Before they had finished this keg, near one third of the town was introduced to this drinking club; they could not pay their part, as they had already disposed of all their skins; but that made no odds—all were welcome to drink.

When they were done with this keg, they applied to the traders, and procured a kettle full of brandy at a time, which they divided out with a large wooden spoon,—and so they went on, and never quit while they had a single beaver skin.

When the trader had got all our beaver, he moved off to the Ottawa town, about a mile above the Wiandot town.

When the brandy was gone, and the drinking club sober, they appeared much dejected. Some of them were crippled, others badly wounded, a number of their fine new shirts tore, and

French Brandy—The encounter Smith's Indian group had with the brandy peddlers was typical. One of the mainstays of the fur trade was alcohol. Although an effort was made to keep it out of the Indian country by some Indian and white leaders who recognized how destructive it was, alcohol remained an important part of the fur trade to the end of the nineteenth century.

At a conference held at Carlisle, Pennsylvania, on October 3, 1753, between representatives of the Pennsylvania governor and chiefs of the Six Nations (Iroquois), Delawares, Shawnees, Twightwees (Miamis), and Owendats (Wyandots), Chief Scarrooyady spoke at length asking for reforms regarding the fur trade in the Ohio country. He was especially emphatic on controlling or eliminating the sale of whiskey by the traders. He said: "These wicked Whiskey Sellers, when they have once got the Indians in liquor, make them sell their very clothes from their backs. In short if this practice be continued, we must be inevitably ruined."

several blankets were burned:—a number of squaws were also in this club, and neglected their corn planting.

We could now hear the effects of the brandy in the Ottawa town. They were singing and yelling in the most hideous manner, both night and day; but their frolic ended worse than ours; five Ottawas were killed and a great many wounded.

After this a number of young Indians were getting their ears cut, and they urged me to have mine cut likewise; but they did not attempt to compel me, though they endeavoured to persuade me. The principal arguments they used were its being a very great ornament, and also the common fashion—The former I did not believe, and the latter I could not deny. The way they performed this operation was by cutting the fleshy part of the circle of the ear close to the gristle quite through. When this was done they wrapt rags round this fleshy part until it was entirely healed; then they hung lead to it and stretched it to a wonderful length: when it was sufficiently stretched, they wrapt the fleshy part round with brass wire, which formed it into a semi circle about four inches diameter.

Many of the young men were now exercising themselves in a game resembling foot ball; though they commonly struck the ball with a crooked stick, made for that purpose; also a game something like this, wherein they used a wooden ball, about three inches diameter, and the instrument they moved it with was a strong staff about five feet

Game resembling foot ball—Most of the Woodland Indians played ball games similar to the ones Smith describes. Sometimes there were hundreds of players on each team and the action was violent. In some games teams composed of women played against the men. There was usually a great deal of betting by the spectators on the outcome of the game. Lacrosse was developed from these Indian ball games.

long, with a hoop net on the end of it,
large enough to contain the ball. Before
they begin the play, they lay off about
half a mile distance in a clear plain,
and the opposite parties all attend at the
centre, where a disinterested person casts
up the ball then the oposite parties all
contend for it. If any one gets it into his
net, he runs with it the way he wishes
it to go, and they all pursue him. If one
of the opposite party overtakes the
person with the ball, he gives the staff
a stroke which causes the ball to fly
out of the net; then they have another
debate for it; and if the one that gets it
can outrun all the opposite party, and
can carry it quite out, or over the line
at the end, the game is won; but this
seldom happens. When any one is running
away with the ball, and is likely to be
overtaken, he commonly throws it, and
with this instrument can cast it fifty
or sixty yards. Sometimes when the ball
is almost at the one end, matters will
take a sudden turn, and the opposite party
may quickly carry it out at the other end.
Often times they will work a long
while back and forward before they can
get the ball over the line, or win the
game.

About the first of June 1757 the
warriors were preparing to go to war, in
the Wiandot, Pottowatomy, and Ottawa
towns; also a great many Jibewas came
down from the upper lakes; and after
singing their war songs and going through
their common ceremonies, they
marched off against the frontiers of
Virginia, Maryland and Pennsylvania,

in their usual manner, singing the
travelling song, slow firing, &c.

On the northside of the river St.
Laurence, opposite to Fort Detroit,
there is an island, which the Indians
call the Long Island, and which they say
is above one thousand miles long, and in
some places above one hundred miles
broad. They further say that the great
river that comes down by Canesatauga
and that empties into the main branch
of St. Laurence, above Montreal,
originates from one source, with the
St. Lawrence, and forms this island.

Opposite to Detroit, and below it, was
originally a prairie, and laid off in lots
about sixty rods broad, and a great length:
each lot is divided into two fields, which
they cultivate year about. The principal
grain that the French raised in these
fields was spring wheat, and peas.

They built all their houses on the front
of these lots on the river side; and as the
banks of the river are very low, some of
the houses are not above three or four
feet above the surface of the water;
yet they are in no danger of being
disturbed by freshes, as the river seldom
rises above eighteen inches; because it is
the communication, of the river St.
Laurence, from one lake to another.

As dwelling-houses, barns, and stables
are all built on the front of these lots;
at a distance it appears like a continued
row of houses in a town, on each side of
the river for a long way. These villages,
the town, the river and the plains,
being all in view at once, afford a most
delightful prospect.

St. Laurence River—
Smith refers in a general
way to the whole system
of the Great Lakes as the
St. Laurence River. The
river which connects
Lakes Erie and St. Clair,
once called the St. Lau-
rence, is now the Detroit
River. Long Island is
most likely western On-
tario.

Great River—*The Ottawa.*

Freshes — refers to a
freshet or sudden high
water, or the overflowing
of a stream.

The inhabitants here chiefly drink the river water; and as it comes from the northward it is very wholesome.

The land here is principally second rate, and comparatively speaking, a small part is first or third rate; tho about four or five miles south of Detroit, their is a small portion that is worse than what I could call third rate, which produces abundance of hurtle berries.

Hurtle berries—These are now called blueberries, which have been variously called whortleberries, hurts, whorts, or bilberries.

There is plenty of good meadow ground here, and a great many marshes that are overspread with water.—The timber is elm, sugar-tree, black-ash, white-ash, abundance of water-ash, oak, hickory, and some walnut.

About the middle of June the Indians were almost all gone to war, from sixteen to sixty; yet Tecaughretanego remained in town with me. Tho he had formerly, when they were at war with the southern nations been a great warrior, and an eminent counsellor; and I think as clear and able a reasoner upon any subject that he had an opportunity of being acquainted with, as I ever knew; yet he had all along been against this war, and had strenuously opposed it in council. He said if the English and French had a quarrel let them fight their own battles themselves; it is not our business to intermeddle therewith.

Southern nations—Most likely the Catawba, Cherokee, Chickasaw, and Creek tribes.

Before the warriors returned we were very scarce of provision: and tho we did not commonly steal from one another; yet we stole during this time any thing that we could eat from the French, under the notion that it was just for us to do so; because they

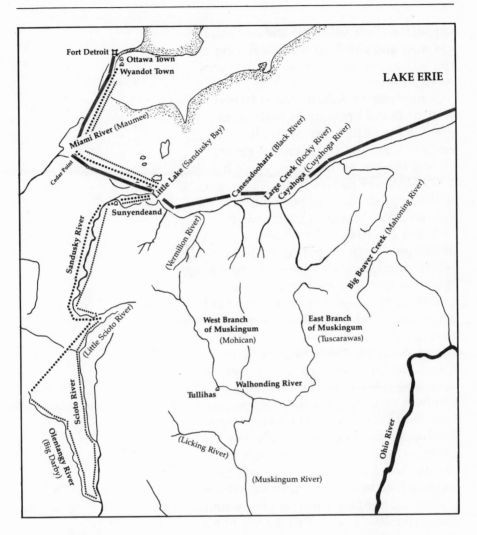

## Map 3

| | | |
|---|---|---|
| [········] | Autumns of 1757 and 1758: | Upstream on the Sandusky River to the Olentangy winter camp. |
| [········] | Springs of 1758 and 1759: | Downstream on the Sandusky to the Wyandot town. |
| [▬▬▬] | Summer, 1759: | East from Fort Detroit to Caughnawaga in Canada. |

supported their soldiers; and our squaws,
old men and children were suffering on
the account of the war, as our hunters
were all gone.

Some time in August the warriors
returned, and brought in with them a
great many scalps, prisoners, horses
and plunder; and the common report
among the young warriors, was, that they
would intirely subdue Tulhasaga, that
is the English, or it might be literally
rendered the Morning Light inhabitants.

About the first of November a number
of families were preparing to go on their
winter hunt, and all agreed to cross the
lake together. We encamped at the
mouth of the river the first night, and a
council was held, whether we should cross
thro' by the three islands, or coast it
round the lake. These islands lie in a line
across the lake, and are just in sight of
each other. Some of the Wiandots or
Ottawas frequently make their winter
hunt on these island. Tho excepting wild
fowl and fish, there is scarcely any game
here but racoons which are amazingly
plenty, and exceedingly large and fat;
as they feed upon the wild rice, which
grows in abundance in wet places round
these islands. It is said that each hunter
in one winter will catch one thousand
racoons.

It is a received opinion among the
Indians that the snakes and racoons are
transmutable; and that a great many of
the snakes turn racoons every fall, and
racoons snakes every spring. This
notion is founded on observations
made on the snakes and racoons in this
island.

As the racoons here lodge in rocks, the trappers make their wooden traps at the mouth of the holes; and as they go daily to look at their traps, in the winter season, they commonly find them filled with racoons; but in the spring or when the frost is out of the ground, they say, they then find their traps filled with large rattle snakes. And therefore conclude that the racoons are transformed. They also say that the reason why they are so remarkably plenty in the winter, is, every fall the snakes turn racoons again.

I told them that tho I had never landed on any of these islands, yet from the unanimous accounts I had received, I believed that both snakes and racoons were plenty there; but no doubt they all remained there both summer and winter, only the snakes were not to be seen in the latter; yet I did not believe that they were transmutable.

These islands are but seldom visited; because early in the spring and late in the fall it is dangerous sailing in their bark canoes; and in the summer they are so infested with various kinds of serpents, (but chiefly rattle snakes,) that it is dangerous landing.

I shall now quit this digression, and return to the result of the council at the mouth of the river. We concluded to coast it round the lake, and in two days we came to the mouth of the Miami of the Lake, and landed on cedar point, where we remained several days. Here we held a council, and concluded

we would take a driving hunt in concert,
and in partnership.

The river in this place is about a mile
broad, and as it and the lake forms a
kind of neck, which terminates in a point,
all the hunters (which were fifty-three)
went up the river, and we scattered
ourselves from the river to the lake.
When we first began to move we were
not in sight of each other, but as we all
raised the yell, we could move regularly
together by the noise. At length we came
in sight of each other and appeared to
be marching in good order; before we
came to the point, both the squaws and
boys in the canoes were scattered up
the river, and along the lake, to prevent
the deer from making their escape by
water. As we advanced near the point the
guns began to crack slowly; and after
some time the firing was like a little
engagement. The squaws and boys were
busy tomahawking the deer in the
water, and we shooting them down on the
land:—We killed in all about thirty
deer: tho a great many made their
escape by water.

We had now great feasting and
rejoicing, as we had plenty of homony,
venison, and wild fowl. The geese at this
time appeared to be preparing to move
southward—It might be asked what is
meant by the geese preparing to move?
The Indians represent them as holding a
great council at this time concerning
the weather in order to conclude upon a
day, that they may all at or near one time
leave the Northern Lakes, and wing their
way to the southern bays. When matters

Council of the wild
geese—It appears to have
been rather common
among American Indian
tribes to attribute near
human traits to wild
animals and birds.
Legends and stories in
Indian tradition about the
buffalo, beaver, wolves,
and coyotes, are charming
and original. The Passa-
maquoddy and the Iro-
quois Indian tales of the
mischievous and daring
Great Rabbit are an
example.

Cedar Point—on Maumee Bay.

Falls of Sandusky—*Rapids at Fremont, Sandusky county, Ohio.*

Wooden canoes — James Smith refers to dugout canoes or pirogues. Made by both Indians and white men, dugouts were in use on the lakes and rivers in the Ohio country until the mid-1800s. While dugouts were not as light-weight and fast as graceful birchbark canoes, they were not as easily damaged either.

Dugouts were hewn from a variety of trees: poplar or tulip, basswood, walnut, white pine, and cypress. The average dugout was twenty to thirty feet in length and twenty to twenty-four inches wide. Large dugouts were made to transport cargoes of trade materials, furs, or household goods.

In 1798 Daniel Boone hewed a dugout sixty feet long from a tulip or poplar log to move his family and possessions down the Big Sandy and Ohio Rivers to Missouri. This dugout had a cargo capacity of about five tons.

are brought to a conclusion, and the time appointed that they are to take wing, then they say, a great number of expresses are sent off, in order to let the different tribes know the result of this council, that they may be all in readiness to move at the time appointed. As there is a great commotion among the geese at this time, it would appear by their actions, that such a council had been held. Certain it is, that they are led by instinct to act in concert and to move off regularly after their leaders.

Here our company separated. The chief part of them went up the Miami river, that empties into Lake Erie, at cedar point, whilst we proceeded on our journey in company with Tecaughretanego, Tontileaugo, and two families of the Wiandots.

As cold weather was now approaching, we began to feel the doleful effects of extravagantly and foolishly spending the large quantity of beaver we had taken in our last winters hunt. We were all nearly in the same circumstances— scarcely one had a shirt to his back; but each of us had an old blanket which we belted round us in the day, and slept in at night, with a deer or bear skin under us for our bed.

When we came to the falls of Sandusky, we buried our birch bark canoes as usual, at a large burying place for that purpose, a little below the falls. At this place the river falls about eight feet over a rock, but not perpendicular. With much difficulty we pushed up our wooden canoes, some of us went up the river,

and the rest by land with the horses,
until we came to the great meadows or
prairies that lie between Sandusky and
Sciota.

When we came to this place we met
with some Ottawa hunters, and agreed
with them to take, what they call a ring
hunt, in partnership. We waited until we
expected rain was near falling to
extinguish the fire, and then we kindled a
large circle in the prairie. At this time,
or before the bucks began to run a great
number of deer lay concealed in the grass,
in the day, and moved about in the night;
but as the fire burned in towards the
centre of the circle, the deer fled before
the fire: the Indians were scattered also
at some distance before the fire, and shot
them down every opportunity, which was
very frequent, especially as the circle
became small. When we came to divide
the deer, there were above ten to each
hunter, which were all killed in a few
hours. The rain did not come on that
night to put out the outside circle of the
fire, and as the wind arose, it extended
thro the whole prairie which was about
fifty miles in length, and in some places
nearly twenty in breadth. This put an
end to our ring hunting this season, and
was in other respects an injury to us in
the hunting business; so that upon the
whole, we received more harm than
benefit by our rapid hunting frolic. We
then moved from the north end of the
glades, and encamped at the carrying
place.

This place is in the plains, betwixt a
creek that empties into Sandusky, and

Prairies—*Formerly known as the Sandusky plains; now within the counties of Crawford, Wyandot, Marion, and Hardin.*

Portage—By the Sandusky, Sciota, and Ohio rivers lay the route of the Indians of Detroit and Lake Huron when going to war with the Catawbas and other southern tribes. "They ascend the Sandusquet river two or three days, after which they make a small portage, a fine road of about a quarter of a league. Some make canoes of elm bark, and float down a small river (the Sciota) that empties into the Ohio." . . . "Through these rivers lies the most common pass from Canada to the Ohio and Mississippi." . . . This once important portage extended from the site of Garrett's Mill, near the village of Wyandot, on the Sandusky river, in Wyandot county; thence south, about four miles on a ridge, through part of Dallas township in Crawford county, to the north branch of the Little Sciota near Swinnerton, on the Old Fort Ball and Columbus road in Grand Prairie township, Marion county. The length of the portage varied according to the stage of water. It was known as the "Four Mile Cross." In high water the north branch of the Little Sciota could be navigated by canoes to a point about a mile distant from Garrett's Mill on the Sandusky. A cut has been made through the ridge about half a mile east from the village of Wyandot, by which the waters of both streams are united.

one that runs into Sciota: and at the time of high water, or in the spring season, there is but about one half mile of portage, and that very level, and clear of rocks, timber or stones; so that with a little digging there may be water carriage the whole way from Sciota to Lake Erie.

From the mouth of Sandusky to the falls is chiefly first rate land, lying flat or level, intermixed with large bodies of clear meadows, where the grass is exceedingly rank, and in many places three or four feet high. The timber is oak, hickory, walnut, cherry, black-ash, elm, sugar-tree, buckeye, locust and beech. In some places there is wet timber land— the timber in these places is chiefly water-ash, sycamore, or button-wood.

From the falls to the prairies, the land lies well to the sun, it is neither too flat nor too hilly—and chiefly first rate. The timber nearly the same as below the falls, excepting the water-ash.—There is also here, some plats of beech land, that appears to be second rate, as it frequently produces spice-wood. The prairie appears to be a tolerably fertile soil, tho in many places too wet for cultivation; yet I apprehend it would produce timber, were it only kept from fire.

The Indians are of the opinion that the squirrels plant all the timber; as they bury a number of nuts for food, and only one at a place. When a squirrel is killed the various kinds of nuts thus buried will grow.

I have observed that when these prairies have only escaped fire for one year, near where a single tree stood, there was a

young growth of timber supposed to be
planted by the squirrels; but when the
prairies were again burned, all this young
growth was immediately consumed; as
the fire rages in the grass, to such a pitch,
that numbers of racoons are thereby
burned to death.

On the west side of the prairie, or
betwixt that and Sciota, there is a large
body of first rate land—the timber, walnut,
locust, sugar-tree, buckeye, cherry, ash,
elm, mulberry, plumb-trees, spicewood,
black-haw, red-haw, oak and hickory.

About the time the bucks quit running,
Tontileaugo his wife and children,
Tecaughretanego, his son Nungany and
myself left the Wiandot camps at the
carrying place, and crossed the Sciota
river at the south end of the glades, and
proceeded on about a south-west course
to a large creek called Ollentangy, which
I believe interlocks with the waters of
the Miami, and empties into Sciota on the
west side thereof, From the south end of
the prairie to Ollentangy, there is a large
quantity of beech land, intermixed with
first rate land. Here we made our winter
hut, and had considerable success in
hunting.

After some time, one of Tontileaugo's
step-sons, (a lad about eight years of age)
offended him, and he gave the boy a
moderate whipping, which much
displeased his Wiandot wife. She
acknowledged that the boy was guilty
of a fault, but thought that he ought to
have been ducked, which is their usual
mode of chastisement. She said she could
not bear to have her son whipped like a

The Ollentangy—By a law
of the Legislature of Ohio,
passed in 1833, "to restore
the Indian names to certain
streams"—this name is incor-
rectly given to the Whet-
stone, the eastern affluent of
the Sciota, the Delaware Indian name of which was
Keenhong-she-consepung,
or Whetstone creek, in
English. . . .

Big Darby creek, which
rises in Logan county and
flowing south-east empties
into the west side of the Sciota
in Pickaway county, opposite
Circleville, is the real Ollentangy; this is clearly evident
from Smith's description of
his route from the Sandusky
portage to that stream, and
of the country between it
and the waters of the Miami
(or Mad river).

The "very large Prairie" is
now embraced within the
counties of Madison, Clarke,
Champaign, Fayette, Pickaway, and Greene, between
Darby creek and Mad river.

Chastisement — Jonathan
Alder was a captive
among the Ohio Indians
during and after the
American Revolution. As
a young boy he lived with
one of his married Indian
sisters, and was badly
mistreated by her, as she
disliked him. When in-
formed that he was being
abused, Jonathan's Indian
mother took him home
after severely reprimand-
ing her daughter. The
deep affection which ex-
isted between the captive
boy and his Indian par-
ents ended only with their
death.

servant or slave—and she was so displeased that when Tontileaugo went out to hunt, she got her two horses, and all her effects, (as in this country the husband and wife have separate interests) and moved back to the Wiandot camps that we had left.

When Tontileaugo returned, he was much disturbed on hearing of his wife's elopement, and said that he would never go after her were it not that he was afraid that she would get bewildered, and that his children that she had taken with her, might suffer. Tontileaugo went after his wife, and when they met they made up the quarrel, and he never returned; but left Tecaughretanego and his son, (a boy about ten years of age) and myself, who remained here in our hut all winter.

Tecaughretanego who had been a first rate warrior, statesman and hunter; and though he was now near sixty years of age, he was yet equal to the common run of hunters, but subject to the rheumatism, which deprived him of the use of his legs.

Shortly after Tontileaugo left us, Tecaughretanego became lame, and could scarcely walk out of our hut for two months. I had considerable success in hunting and trapping. Though Tecaughretanego endured much pain and misery, yet he bore it all with wonderful patience, and would often endeavor to entertain me with chearful conversation. Some times he would applaud me for my diligence, skill and activity—and at other times he would take great care in giving me instructions concerning the hunting

and trapping business. He would also tell
me that if I failed of success, we would
suffer very much, as we were about forty
miles from any one living, that we knew
of; yet he would not intimate that he
apprehended we were in any danger,
but still supposed that I was fully
adequate to the task.

Tontileaugo left us a little before
Christmas, and from that until some time
in February, we had always plenty of
bear meat, venison, &c. During this time
I killed much more than we could use,
but having no horses to carry in what I
killed, I left part of it in the woods. In
February there came a snow, with a crust,
which made a great noise when walking
on it, and frightened away the deer; and
as bear and beaver were scarce here, we
got entirely out of provision. After I had
hunted two days without eating any
thing, and had very short allowance for
some days before, I returned late in the
evening faint and weary. When I came
into our hut, Tecaughretanego asked
what success? I told him not any. He
asked me if I was not very hungry? I
replied that the keen appetite seemed
to be in some measure removed, but I
was both faint and weary. He commanded
Nunganey his little son, to bring me
something to eat, and he brought me a
kettle with some bones and broth,—
after eating a few mouthfuls, my appetite
violently returned, and I thought the
victuals had a most agreable relish,
though it was only fox and wild-cat bones,
which lay about the camp, which the
ravens and turkey-buzzards had picked—

these Nunganey had collected and
boiled, until the sinews that remained on
the bones would strip off. I speedily
finished my allowance, such as it was,
and when I had ended my sweet repast,
Tecaughretanego asked me how I felt?
I told him that I was much refreshed. He
then handed me his pipe and pouch, and
told me to take a smoke. I did so. He then
said he had something of importance to
tell me, if I was now composed and ready
to hear it. I told him that I was ready to
hear him. He said the reason why he
deferred his speech till now, was because
few men are in a right humor to hear
good talk, when they are extremely
hungry, as they are then generally fretful
and discomposed; but as you appear now
to enjoy calmness and serenity of mind,
I will now communicate to you the
thoughts of my heart, and those things
that I know to be true.

"Brother,

"As you have lived with the white
people, you have not had the same
advantage of knowing that the great being
above feeds his people, and gives them
their meat in due season, as we Indians
have, who are frequently out of
provisions, and yet are wonderfully
supplied, and that so frequently that it
is evidently the hand of the great
Owaneeyo* that doth this: whereas the
white people have commonly large stocks
of tame cattle, that they can kill when
they please, and also their barns and
cribs filled with grain, and therefore

* This is the name of God, in their tongue, and
signifies the owner and ruler of all things.

have not the same opportunity of seeing
and knowing that they are supported by
the ruler of Heaven and Earth.

"Brother,

"I know that you are now afraid that
we will all perish with hunger, but you
have no just reason to fear this.

"Brother,

"I have been young, but am now old
—I have been frequently under the like
circumstances that we now are, and that
some time or other in almost every year
of my life; yet, I have hitherto been
supported, and my wants supplied in time
of need.

"Brother,

"Owaneeyo sometimes suffers us to be
in want, in order to teach us our
dependance upon him, and to let us
know that we are to love and serve him:
and likewise to know the worth of the
favors that we receive, and to make us
more thankful.

"Brother,

"Be assured that you will be supplied
with food, and that just in the right time;
but you must continue diligent in the use
of means—go to sleep, and rise early in the
morning and go a hunting—be strong and
exert yourself like a man, and the great
spirit will direct your way."

The next morning I went out, and
steered about an east course. I
proceeded on slowly for about five
miles, and saw deer frequently, but as
the crust on the snow made a great noise,
they were always running before I spied
them, so that I could not get a shoot. A
violent appetite returned, and I became

intolerably hungry;—it was now that I concluded I would run off to Pennsylvania, my native country. As the snow was on the ground, the Indian hunters almost the whole of the way before me, I had but a poor prospect of making my escape, but my case appeared desperate. If I staid here I thought I would perish with hunger, and if I met with Indians, they could but kill me.

I then proceeded on as fast as I could walk, and when I got about ten or twelve miles from our hut, I came upon fresh buffaloe tracks,—I pursued after, and in a short time came in sight of them, as they were passing through a small glade—I ran with all my might, and headed them, where I lay in ambush, and killed a very large cow. I immediately kindled a fire and began to roast meat, but could not wait till it was done—I ate it almost raw. When hunger was abated I began to be tenderly concerned for my old Indian brother, and the little boy I had left in a perishing condition. I made haste and packed up what meat I could carry, secured what I left from the wolves, and returned homewards.

I scarcely thought on the old man's speech while I was almost distracted with hunger, but on my return was much affected with it, reflected on myself for my hard-heartedness and ingratitude, in attempting to run off and leave the venerable old man and little boy to perish with hunger. I also considered how remarkably the old man's speech had been verified in our providentially obtaining a supply. I thought also of that

Secured . . . from the wolves—All hunters had the problem of storing the meat of a big animal killed in the woods until it could be transported to camp. The buffalo cow Smith killed was too large for him to take back in one trip. To keep it from the wolves, he butchered the cow into pieces he could handle and put these into the trees out of the wolves' reach.

If he had to tie the meat in place, Smith could have used strips of green tree bark or cut strips from rawhide with his tomahawk. In winter, there was no problem of spoilage.

part of his speech which treated of the
fractious dispositions of hungry people,
which was the only excuse I had for my
base inhumanity, in attempting to leave
them in the most deplorable situation.

As it was moon-light, I got home to our
hut, and found the old man in his usual
good humor. He thanked me for my
exertion, and bid me sit down, as I
must certainly be fatigued, and he
commanded Nunganey to make haste and
cook. I told him I would cook for him,
and let the boy lay some meat on the
coals, for himself—which he did, but
ate it almost raw, as I had done. I
immediately hung on the kettle with
some water, and cut the beef in thin
slices, and put them in:—when it
had boiled awhile, I proposed taking
it off the fire, but the old man replied,
"let it be done enough." This he said in
as patient and unconcerned a manner,
as if he had not wanted one single meal.
He commanded Nunganey to eat no more
beef at that time, least he might hurt
himself; but told him to sit down, and
after some time he might sup some
broth—this command he reluctantly
obeyed.

When we were all refreshed,
Tecaughretanego delivered a speech
upon the necessity and pleasure of
receiving the necessary supports of life
with thankfulness, knowing that
Owaneeyo is the great giver. Such
speeches from an Indian, may be tho't
by those who are unacquainted with
them, altogether incredible; but when
we reflect on the Indian war, we may

readily conclude that they are not an
ignorant or stupid sort of people, or
they would not have been such fatal
enemies. When they came into our
country they outwitted us—and when
we sent armies into their country, they
outgeneralled, and beat us with inferior
force. Let us also take into consideration
that Tecaughretanego was no common
person, but was among the Indians, as
Socrates in the ancient Heathen world;
and it may be, equal to him—if not in
wisdom and in learning, yet, perhaps, in
patience and fortitude. Notwithstanding
Tecauretanego's, uncommon natural
abilitis, yet in the sequel of this history
you will see the deficiency of the light
of nature, unaided by revelation, in this
truly great man.

The next morning Tecaughretanego
desired me to go back and bring another
load of buffaloe beef: As I proceeded
to do so, about five miles from our hut
I found a bear tree. As a sapling, grew
near the tree, and reached near the hole
that the bear went in at, I got dry dozed
or rotton wood, that would catch and hold
fire as well as spunk. This wood I tied
up in bunches, fixed them on my back,
and then climbed up the sapling, and with
a pole I put them touched with fire,
into the hole, and then came down and
took my gun in my hand. After some time
the bear came out, and I killed and
skinned it, packed up a load of the meat,
(after securing the remainder from
the wolves) and returned home before
night. On my return my old brother
and his son were much rejoiced at my

success. After this we had plenty of
provision.

We remained here until some time
in April 1758. At this time Tecaughretanego
had recovered so, that he could walk
about. We made a bark canoe, embarked,
and went down Ollentangy some distance,
but the water being low, we were in
danger of splitting our canoe upon the
rocks: therefore Tecaughretanego
concluded we would encamp on shore,
and pray for rain.

When we encamped, Tecaughretanego
made himself a sweat-house; which he did
by sticking a number of hoops in the
ground, each hoop forming a semi-
circle—this he covered all round with
blankets and skins; he then prepared hot
stones, which he rolled into this hut,
and then went into it himself, with a
little kettle of water in his hand, mixed
with a variety of herbs, which he had
formerly cured, and had now with him
in his pack—they afforded an odoriferous
perfume. When he was in, he told me to
pull down the blankets behind him,
and cover all up close, which I did, and
then he began to pour water upon the
hot stones, and to sing aloud. He
continued in this vehement hot place
about fifteen minutes:—all this he
did in order to purify himself before he
would address the Supreme Being.
When he came out of his sweat-house,
he began to burn tobacco and pray.
He began each petition with <u>oh</u>, <u>ho</u>, <u>ho</u>,
<u>ho</u>, which is a kind of aspiration, and
signifies an ardent wish. I observed
that all his petitions were only for

Sweat-house—The sweat-
bath was used by the In-
dians in many parts of
America for both physi-
cal and spiritual purifica-
tion. It combined medi-
cinal and religious
elements in a ritual that
was somewhat difficult for
a non-Indian to com-
pletely understand. The
sweat-house ceremony
is still in use by some
plains Indians today—
the Sioux, Cheyenne,
Blackfeet, and Crows
among others.

immediate or present temporal blessings.
He began his address by thanksgiving,
in the following manner:

"O great being! I thank thee that I
have obtained the use of my legs again
—that I am now able to walk about and
kill turkeys, &c. without feeling exquisite
pain and misery: I know that thou art a
hearer and a helper, and therefore I will
call upon thee.

"Oh, ho, ho, ho,

"Grant that my knees and ankles may
be right well, and that I may be able,
not only to walk, but to run, and to
jump logs, as I did last fall.

"Oh, ho, ho, ho,

"Grant that on this voyage we may
frequently kill bears, as they may be
crossing the Sciota and Sandusky.

"Oh, ho, ho, ho,

"Grant that we may kill plenty of
Turkeys along the banks, to stew with
our fat bear meat.

"Oh, ho, ho, ho,

"Grant that rain may come to raise
the Ollentangy about two or three feet,
that we may cross in safety down to
Sciota, without danger of our canoe
being wrecked on the rocks:—and
now, O great being! thou knowest how
matters stand—thou knowest that
I am a great lover of tobacco, and though
I know not when I may get any more,
I now make a present of the last I have
unto thee, as a free burnt offering;
therefore I expect thou wilt hear and
grant these requests, and I thy servant
will return thee thanks, and love thee
for thy gifts."

During the whole of this scene I sat
by Tecaughretanego, and as he went
through it with the greatest solemnity,
I was seriously affected with his prayers.
I remained duly composed until he came
to the burning of the tobacco, and as I
knew that he was a great lover of it,
and saw him cast the last of it into the
fire, it excited in me a kind of meriment,
and I insensibly smiled. Tecaughretanego
observed me laughing, which displeased
him, and occasioned him to address me in
the following manner.
    "Brother,
"I have somewhat to say to you, and I
hope you will not be offended when I
tell you of your faults. You know that
when you were reading your books in
town, I would not let the boys or any
one disturb you; but now when I was
praying, I saw you laughing. I do not
think that you look upon praying as a
foolish thing;—I believe you pray yourself.
But perhaps you may think my mode, or
manner of praying foolish; if so, you
ought in a friendly manner to instruct
me, and not make sport of sacred things."
    I acknowledged my error, and on
this he handed me his pipe to smoke,
in token of friendship and reconciliation;
though at this time he had nothing to
smoke, but red-willow bark. I told him
something of the method of reconciliation
with an offended God, as revealed in
my Bible, which I had then in possession.
He said that he liked my story better
than that of the French priests, but he
thought that he was now too old to begin
to learn a new religion, therefore he

should continue to worship God in the
way that he had been taught, and that
if salvation or future happiness was to
be had in his way of worship, he expected
he would obtain it, and if it was
inconsistent with the honor of the great
spirit to accept of him in his own way of
worship, he hoped that Owaneeyo would
accept of him in the way I had
mentioned, or in some other way,
though he might now be ignorant of the
channel through which favor or mercy
might be conveyed. He said that he
believed that Owaneeyo would hear
and help every one that sincerely waited
upon him.

Here we may see how far the light of
nature could go; perhaps we see it here
almost in its highest extent. Notwithstanding the just views that this great man
entertained of Providence, yet we now
see him (though he acknowledged
his guilt) expecting to appease the
Deity, and procure his favor, by burning
a little tobacco. We may observe that all
Heathen nations, as far as we can find
out either by tradition or the light of
Nature, agree with Revelation in this,
that sacrifice is necessary, or that some
kind of attonement is to be made, in
order to remove guilt, and reconcile
them to God. This, accompanied with
numberless other witnesses, is sufficient
evidence of the rationality of the truth
of the Scriptures.

A few days after Tecaughretanego
had gone through his ceremonies, and
finished his prayers, the rain came and
raised the creek a sufficient height, so

that we passed in safety down to Sciota,
and proceeded up to the carrying place.
Let us now describe the land on this
route, from our winter hut, and down
Ollentangy to the Sciota, and up it to
the carrying place.

About our winter cabbin is chiefly
first and second rate land. A considerable
way up Ollentangy on the south-west
side thereof, or betwixt it and the Miami,
there is a very large prairie, and from this
prairie down Ollentangy to Sciota, is
generally first rate land. The timber is
walnut, sugar-tree, ash, buckeye, locust,
wild cherry and spice-wood, intermixed
with some oak and beech. From the
mouth of Ollentangy on the east side of
Sciota, up to the carrying place, there
is a large body of first and second rate
land, and tolerably well watered. The
timber is ash, sugar-tree, walnut locust,
oak, and beech. Up near the carrying
place the land is a little hilly, but the soil
good.

We proceeded from this place down
Sandusky, and in our passage we killed
four bears, and a number of turkeys.
Tecaughretanego appeared now fully
persuaded that all this came in answer
to his prayers—and who can say with
any degree of certainty that it was not so?

When we came to the little lake at the
mouth of Sandusky we called at a
Wiandot town that was then there, called
Sunyendeand. Here we diverted
ourselves several days, by catching
rock-fish in a small creek, the name of
which is also Sunyendeand, which
signifies Rock-Fish. They fished in the

Rock−fish — These fish
were most probably large
mouth black bass.

night, with lights, and struck the fish
with giggs or spears. The rock-fish here,
when they begin first to run up the creek
to spawn, are exceedingly fat, sufficient
to fry themselves. The first night we
scarcely caught fish enough for present
use, for all that was in the town.

The next morning I met with a prisoner
at this place, by the name of Thompson,
who had been taken from Virginia: he
told me if the Indians would only omit
disturbing the fish for one night, he
could catch more fish than the whole
town could make use of. I told Mr.
Thompson that if he was certain he could
do this, that I would use my influence
with the Indians, to let the fish alone
for one night. I applied to the chiefs,
who agreed to my proposal, and said they
were anxious to see what the Great
Knife (as they called the Virginian)
could do. Mr. Thompson, with the
assistance of some other prisoners, set
to work, and made a hoop net of Elm
bark: they then cut down a tree across
the creek, and stuck in stakes at the
lower side of it, to prevent the fish from
passing up, leaving only a gap at the one
side of the creek:—here he sat with his
net, and when he felt the fish touch the
net he drew it up, and frequently would
hawl out two or three rock-fish that would
weigh about five or six pounds each. He
continued at this until he had hawled out
about a waggon load, and then left the
gap open, in order to let them pass up,
for they could not go far, on account of
the shallow water. Before day Mr.
Thompson shut it up, to prevent them

from passing down, in order to let the
Indians have some diversion in killing
them in daylight.

When the news of the fish came to town,
the Indians all collected, and with
surprize beheld the large heap of fish,
and applauded the ingenuity of the
Virginian. When they saw the number of
them that were confined in the water
above the tree, the young Indians ran
back to the town, and in a short time
returned with their spears, giggs, bows
and arrows, &c. and were the chief of
that day engaged in killing rock-fish,
insomuch that we had more than we
could use or preserve. As we had no
salt, or any way to keep them, they lay
upon the banks, and after some time
great numbers of turkey-buzzards and
eagles collected together and devoured
them.

Shortly after this we left Sunyendeand,
and in three days arrived at Detroit,
where we remained this summer.

Some time in May we heard that
General Forbes, with seven thousand men
was preparing to carry on a campaign
against Fort DuQuesne, which then stood
near where Fort Pitt was afterwards
erected. Upon receiving this news a
number of runners were sent off by the
French commander at Detroit, to urge
the different tribes of Indian warriors to
repair to Fort DuQuesne.

Some time in July 1758, the Ottowas,
Jibewas, Potowatomies, and Wiandots,
rendzvouzed at Detroit, and marched off
to Fort DuQuesne, to prepare for the
encounter of General Forbes. The common

Colonel Grant—*Grant's defeat and capture took place on the 14th day of September, 1758. He was a Major General in the British service during the American Revolution. He was promoted to the rank of Lieutenant General in 1782, and General in 1796, and died "very old," at his seat at Ballendallock, near Elgin in Scotland, about the 13th of May, 1806. . . . The court house in Pittsburg, fronting on Grant street, stands near the western extremity of the once beautiful eminence called "Grant's Hill," which long since has been graded and covered with buildings.*

report was, that they would serve him as they did General Braddock, and obtain much plunder. From this time, until fall, we had frequent account of Forbes's army, by Indian runners that were sent out to watch their motion. They spied them frequently from the mountains ever after they left Fort Loudon. Notwithstanding their vigilence, colonel Grant with his Highlanders stole a march upon them, and in the night took possession of a hill about eighty rod from Fort DuQuesne: —this hill is on that account called Grant's hill to this day. The French and Indians knew not that Grant and his men were there until they beat the drum and played upon the bagpipes, just at day-light. They then flew to arms, and the Indians ran up under covert of the banks of Allegheny and Monongahela, for some distance, and then sallied out from the banks of the rivers, and took possession of the hill above Grant; and as he was on the point of it in sight of the fort, they immediately surrounded him, and as he had his Highlanders in ranks, and in very close order, and the Indians scattered, and concealed behind trees, they defeated him with the loss only of a few warriors: —most of the Highlanders were killed or taken prisoners.

After this defeat the Indians held a council, but were divided in their opinions. Some said that general Forbes would now turn back, and go home the way that he came, as Dunbar had done when General Braddock was defeated: others supposed he would come on. The French urged the Indians to stay and

see the event: but as it was hard for the
Indians to be absent from their squaws
and children, at this season of the year, a
great many of them returned home to
their hunting. After this, the remainder
of the Indians, some French regulars, and
a number of Canadians, marched off in
quest of General Forbes. They met his
army near Fort Ligoneer, and attacked
them, but were frustrated in their design.
They said that Forbes's men were
beginning to learn the art of war, and
that there were a great number of
American riflemen along with the
read-coats, who scattered out, took trees,
and were good marks-men; therefore they
found they could not accomplish their
design, and were obliged to retreat.
When they returned from the battle to
Fort DuQuesne, the Indians conclued
that they would go to their hunting. The
French endeavored to persuade them to
stay and try another battle. The Indians
said if it was only the red-coats they had
to do with, they could soon subdue them,
but they could not withstand <u>Ashalecoa</u>,
or the Great Knife, which was the name
they gave the Virginians. They then
returned home to their hunting, and the
French evacuated the fort, which General
Forbes came and took possession of
without further opposition, late in the
year 1758, and at this time began to
build Fort Pitt.

When Tecaughretanego had heard the
particulars of Grant's defeat, he said that
he could now well account for his
contradictory and inconsistent conduct.
He said as the art of war consists in

ambushing and surprizing our enemies, and in preventing them from ambushing and surprizing us; Grant, in the first place, acted like a wise and experienced officer, in artfully approaching in the night without being discovered; but when he came to the place, and the Indians were lying asleep outside of the fort, between him and the Allegheny river, in place of slipping up quietly, and falling upon them with their broad swords, they beat the drums and played upon the bagpipes. He said he could account for this inconsistent conduct no other way than by supposing that he had made too free with spirituous liquors during the night, and became intoxicated about day-light. But to return:

This year we hunted up Sandusky, and down Sciota, and took nearly the same route that we had done the last hunting season. We had considerable success, and returned to Detroit some time in April 1759.

Shortly after this, Tecaughretanego, his son Nungany and myself, went from Detroit, (in an elm bark canoe) to Caughnewaga, a very ancient Indian town, about nine miles above Montreal, where I remained until about the first of July. I then heard of a French ship at Montreal that had English prisoners on board, in order to carry them over sea, and exchange them. I went privately off from the Indians, and got also on board; but as general Wolfe had stopped the River St. Laurence, we were all sent to prison in Montreal, where I remained four months. Some time in November we

Caughnawaga—This old Mohawk town still exists on the St. Lawrence River at Montreal. It was a long canoe trip that Smith, Tecaughretanego, and Nungany made down Lakes Erie and Ontario, and the St. Lawrence— probably seven or eight hundred miles.

were all sent off from this place to Crown Point, and exchanged.

Early in the year 1760, I came home to Canacocheague, and found that my people could never ascertain whether I was killed or taken, until my return. They received me with great joy, but were surprized to see me so much like an Indian, both in my gait and gesture.

Upon enquiry, I found that my sweetheart was married a few days before I arrived. My feelings I must leave on this occasion, for those of my readers to judge, who have felt the pangs of disappointed love, as it is impossible now for me to describe the emotion of soul I felt at that time.

Now there was peace with the Indians which lasted until the year 1763. Some time in May, this year, I married, and about that time the Indians again commenced hostilities, and were busily engaged in killing and scalping the frontier inhabitants in various parts of Pennsylvania. The whole Conococheague Valley, from the North to the South Mountain, had been almost entirely evacuated during Braddock's war. This state was then a Quaker government, and at the first of this war the frontiers received no assistance from the state. As the people were now beginning to live at home again, they thought hard to be drove away a second time, and were determined if possible, to make a stand; therefore they raised as much money by collections and subscriptions, as would pay a company of rifle-men for several months. The subscribers met and elected

Crown Point—This point was located on the west side and near the lower end of Lake Champlain in New York. The English had a trading post there, on the route between Canada and New York, in the early eighteenth century.

The Crown Point area was important to both France and England in their struggle for America. France built Fort Frederic there in 1731. About ten miles south they later built Fort Ticonderoga. In 1759 Lord Amherst took Fort Frederic and rebuilt the French fortification, naming it Crown Point. Much fighting took place between English, French, and Indian forces in this historic area.

Indian hostilities of 1763 —These were part of Pontiac's War, also known as the Conspiracy of Pontiac. This was a well coordinated effort by the Indians to drive the English out of the Ohio and Great Lakes country.

Pontiac was an Ottawa chief about fifty years of age. Although not much is known about his early life, Pontiac was a natural leader and orator with military experience in the French and Indian War. He was said to have taken part in Braddock's defeat in 1755.

Pontiac was able to organize the Indians in a series of surprise attacks on British forts in May and June 1763, that resulted in the capture or destruction of eight forts in the Great Lakes and Ohio country. Fort La-

Baye at Green Bay, Wisconsin, was evacuated; two important posts, Fort Detroit and Fort Pitt, were besieged for months but successfully held off the Indians.

Pontiac's War was remarkable for the concerted effort of the various tribes involved over a vast area. In September 1763 the Indians attacked Fort Niagara, about five hundred miles east of Green Bay. It did not fall, but suffered severe casualties.

Indian war parties continued raiding Pennsylvania and Virginia, driving out and killing hundreds of settlers. Smith and his company of scouts, the "black boys," must have seen a great deal of service during the war, but he writes rather sparingly of their experiences. Pontiac's forces inflicted about 300 casualties on the British before the war ended. The Indian losses were much less.

**Susquehannah Campaign** —*In September and October, 1763, the Indian villages destroyed stood on the Great Island and on the banks of the Susquehannah river, in the present counties of Clinton and Lycoming.*

**Gen. Bouquet's Campaign** —*The hostages were fourteen in number; two Mingoes, six Delawares, and six Shawnees. Only the latter escaped on the way to Fort Pitt. The others being unconfined afterward disappeared, excepting three. The prisoners held by the Shawnees were collected during the winter and brought*

a committee to manage the business. The committee appointed me captain of this company of rangers, and gave me the appointment of my subalterns. I chose two of the most active young men that I could find, who had also been long in captivity with the Indians. As we enlisted our men, we dressed them uniformly in the Indian manner, with breech-clouts, leggins, mockesons, and green shrouds, which we wore in the same manner that the Indians do, and nearly as the Highlanders wear their plaids. In place of hats we wore red handkerchiefs, and painted our faces red and black, like Indian warriors. I taught them the Indian discipline, as I knew of no other at that time, which would answer the purpose much better than British. We succeeded beyond expectation in defending the frontiers, and were extolled by our employers. Near the conclusion of this expedition I accepted of an ensign's commission in the regular service, under King George, in what was then called the Pennsylvania line. Upon my resignation, my lieutenant succeeded me in command, the rest of the time they were to serve. In the fall (the same year) I went on the Susquehannah campaign, against the Indians, under the command of General Armstrong. In this route we burnt the Delaware and Monsey towns, on the West Branch of the Susquehannah, and destroyed all their corn.

In the year 1764, I received a lieutenant's commission, and went out on General Bouquet's campaign against the Indians on the Muskingum. Here we brought them to terms, and promised to be at peace with them, upon condition that they would give up all our people that they had then in captivity among them. They then delivered unto us three hundred of the prisoners, and said that they could not collect them all at this time, as it was now late in the year, and they were far scattered; but they promised that they would bring them all into Fort Pitt early next spring, and as security that they would do this, they delivered to us six of their chiefs, as hostages. Upon this we settled a cessation of arms for six months, and promised upon their fulfilling the aforesaid condition, to make with them a permanent peace.

A little below Fort Pitt the hostages all made their escape. Shortly after this the Indians stole horses, and killed some people on the frontiers. The king's proclamation was then circulating and set up in various public places, prohibiting any person from trading with the Indians, until further orders.

Notwithstanding all this, about the first of March 1765, a number of waggons loaded with Indian goods, and warlike stores, were sent from Philadelphia to Henry Pollens's, Conococheague, and from thence seventy pack-horses were loaded with these goods, in order to carry them to Fort Pitt. This alarmed the country, and Mr. William Duffield raised about fifty armed men, and met the pack-horses at the place where Mercersburg now stands. Mr. Duffield desired the employers to store up their goods, and

to Fort Pitt (in May, 1765), where five hundred and seventy-one chiefs and warriors (besides women and children,) assembled and held a friendly conference with Major Murray and the officers of the garrison. The treaty made with Gen. Bouquet the preceding November at the Muskingum was formally ratified. One hundred and nineteen Shawnee warriors were present. . . .

Katepacomen (or Simon Girty), was one of the Delaware hostages. It appears that upon one occasion, during the campaign, the Shawnees selected James Smith to represent them. . . .

In 1764 Colonel Bouquet erected a brick redoubt as an addition to Fort Pitt. It is yet standing, and used for a dwelling house. The stone tablet in the wall, bearing the inscription, Coll. Bouquet, A.D. 1764, has been removed recently and placed in the wall of the new city hall. This redoubt is the only relic of British dominion in the Ohio valley.

The governor and council of Pennsylvania, uncertain of the consequences of the escape of the Shawnee hostages, deferred proclaiming the Indian trade opened according to the royal proclamation of October 7th; 1763, until notified by Sir William Johnson that a general peace had been concluded with the Western Indians. . . . At the conferences at the Muskingum and Fort Pitt the Indians expressed their anxiety for the beginning of trade, and were displeased when it was refused. . . . General Gage was anxious to have the trade commence, fearing the Indians would again resort to the French. . . . Governor Penn's proclamation declaring the Indian trade opened to licensed traders was issued on June 4, 1765.

The Conococheague settlement, now Franklin county, Pennsylvania, being on the extreme frontier, suffered repeatedly all the horrors of Indian warfare. The settlers were Scots-Irish Presbyterians, who "though neglected by the royal and provincial governments throughout all the Indian wars sustained nearly the whole burden of defending the frontier." . . . . "Two hundred miles of an extended frontier all so exposed to the incursions of the Indians, that no man can go to sleep within ten or fifteen miles of the border without danger of having his house burned and himself and family scalped or led into captivity before the next morning." . . . .

The policy of the governor and the commander-in-chief, Gage, was not understood or appreciated by the people of the frontier, and they determined on their only preventive course. Their leader was James Smith, who was "a man of resolution, of indomitable courage, and inflexible from any purpose which he deemed necessary for the safety of the inhabitants."

His family were prominent in the county from its earliest settlement. "Smith's," now Mercersburg, "was in early days an important place for trade with the Indians and settlers on the Western frontier." . . . .

The traders' goods were destroyed, as related in the narrative and in a letter from Colonel Reid commanding the district of Fort Pitt. . . . .

The convoy was in charge of Captain Robert Callender, an old trader. It consisted of

not proceed until further orders. They made light of this, and went over the North Mountain, where they lodged in a small valley called the Great Cove. Mr. Duffield and his party followed after, and came to their lodging, and again urged them to store up their goods:— He reasoned with them on the impropriety of their proceedings, and the great danger the frontier inhabitants would be exposed to, if the Indians should now get a supply:—He said as it was well known that they had scarcely any ammunition, and were almost naked, to supply them now, would be a kind of murder, and would be illegally trading at the expence of the blood and treasure of the frontiers. Notwithstanding his powerful reasoning, these traders made game of what he said, and would only answer him by ludicrous burlesque.

When I beheld this, and found that Mr. Duffield would not compel them to store up their goods, I collected ten of my old warriors, that I had formerly disciplined in the Indian way, went off privately, after night, and encamped in the woods. The next day, as usual, we blacked and painted, and waylayed them near Sidelong Hill. I scattered my men about forty rod along the side of the road and ordered every two to take a tree, and about eight or ten rod between each couple, with orders to keep a reserve fire, one not to fire until his comrade had loaded his gun—by this means we kept up a constant, slow fire, upon them, from front to rear.—We then heard nothing of these trader's merriment or burlesque.

When they saw their pack-horses falling close by them, they called out <u>pray, gentlemen, what would you have us to do?</u> The reply was, <u>collect all your loads to the front, and unload them in one place; take your private property, and immediately retire</u>. When they were gone, we burnt what they left, which consisted of blankets, shirts, vermillion, lead, beads, wampum, tomahawks, scalping knives, &c.

The traders went back to Fort Loudon, and applied to the commanding officer there, and got a party of Highland soldiers, and went with them in quest of the robbers, as they called us, and without applying to a magistrate, or obtaining any civil authority, but barely upon suspicion, they took a number of creditable persons prisoners, (who were chiefly not any way concerned in this action) and confined them in the guard-house in Fort Loudon. I then raised three hundred riflemen, marched to Fort Loudon, and encamped on a hill in sight of the fort. We were not long there, until we had more than double as many of the British troops prisoners in our camp, as they had of our people in the guard-house. Captain Grant, a Highland officer, who commanded Fort Loudon, then sent a flag of truce to our camp, where we settled a cartel, and gave them above two for one, which enabled us to redeem all our men from the guard-house, without further difficulty.

After this, Captain Grant kept a number of rifle guns, which the Highlanders had taken from the country people, and

*eighty-one horse loads, sixty-three of which were destroyed.*

*The affair caused a great sensation throughout the province. The goods, valued at £3,000, belonged to Baynton, Wharton and Morgan, who alleged they were destined for the Illinois and to be stored at Fort Pitt. . . .*

*General Gage was likewise "of the opinion" that "the traders had hopes of getting first to market by stealing up their goods before the trade was legally permitted." . . . During this summer traders' goods were not allowed to go forward without a pass from William or James Smith. The following is a copy of one:*

*"As the Sidling hill volunteers have already inspected these goods, and as they are all private property, it is expected that none of these brave fellows will molest them upon the road, as there is no Indian supplies amongst them. Given under my hand, May 15, 1765.*

*"(Signed) JAS. SMITH."*

*The governor by the advice of the council, on Jan. 15, 1766, removed William Smith from the magistracy, and directed the chief justice to issue a writ for the apprehension of James, . . . It does not appear that any attempt was ever made to execute the writ, although it was issued to the sheriff of Cumberland county.*

Sideling Hill—*A low ridge of the Allegheny mountains in Fulton county. The foot of the hill is about sixteen miles east of the town of Bedford. The road across it, seven miles in length, is well remembered by travellers as tedious, and often dangerous.*

Forty rod—Approximately the length of two football fields.

Affairs at Fort Loudon—*Lieutenant Charles Grant of the 42d Highland regiment commanded at Fort Loudon. The following characteristic letter was sent to him by Smith:*

Smith's Run, June 19, 1765.
Sir: The arms that are detained in Loudon you may keep them, keep them, keep them! I am, etc.,
JAMES SMITH

*In November, Lieutenant Grant having taken more arms from the country people, and being ordered to Fort Pitt to compel a surrender of the guns, the riflemen headed by Smith besieged Fort Loudon for two days and nights, so closely, that no one was permitted to go in or out of it. Firing was kept up "upon all corners of the fort, so that the centrys could not stand upright on the bastions." No one was 'urt on either side. On the ᵗh of November the guns were surrendered to the custody of Wm. McDowell "until the governor's pleasure respecting them should be known." The arms were "five rifles and four smooth bored guns."*

refused to give them up. As he was riding out one day, we took him prisoner, and detained him until he delivered up the arms; we also destroyed a large quantity of gun-powder that the traders had stored up, lest it might be conveyed privately to the Indians. The king's troops, and our party, had now got entirely out of the channel of the civil law, and many unjustifiable things were done by both parties. This convinced me more than ever I had been before, of the absolute necessity of the civil law, in order to govern mankind.

About this time, the following song was composed by Mr. George Campbell, (an Irish gentleman, who had been educated in Dublin) and was frequently sung to the tune of the Black Joke.

1. Ye patriot souls who love to sing,
   What serves your country and your king,
      In wealth, peace and royal estate;
   Attention give, whilst I rehearse
   A modern fact, in jingling verse,
   How party interest strove what it cou'd,
   To profit itself by public blood,
      But justly met its merited fate.

2. Let all those Indian traders claim,
   Their just reward, inglorious fame,
      For vile base and treacherous ends.
   To Pollins, in the spring they sent,
   Much warlike stores, with an intent,
   To carry them to our barbarous foes,
   Expecting that no-body dare oppose,
      A present to their Indian friends.

3. Astonish'd at the wild design,
   Frontier inhabitants combin'd,
      With brave souls, to stop their career,
   Although some men apostatiz'd,
   Who first the grand attempt advis'd,
   The bold frontiers they bravely stood,

> To act for their king and their country's
> good,
>> In joint league, and strangers to
>> fear.

4. On March the fifth, in sixty-five,
The Indian presents did arrive,
> In long pomp and cavalcade,
Near Sidelong Hill, where in disguise,
Some patriots did their train surprize,
And quick as lightning tumbled ther
loads,
And kindled them bonfires in the woods,
> And mostly burnt their whole brigade.

5. At Loudon, when they heard the news,
They scarcely knew which way to
choose,
> For blind rage and discontent;
At length some soldiers they sent out,
With guides for to conduct the route,
And seized some men that were
trav'ling there,
And hurried them into Loudon where
> They laid them fast with one
> consent.

6. But men of resolution thought,
Too much to see their neighbours
caught,
> For no crime but false surmise;
Forthwith they join'd a warlike band,
And march'd to Loudon out of hand,
And kept the jailers pris'ners there,
Until our friends enlarged were,
> Without fraud or any disguise.

7. Let mankind censure or commend,
This rash performance in the end,
> Then both sides will find their
> account.
'Tis true no law can justify,
To burn our neighbors property,
But when this property is design'd,
To serve the enemies of mankind,
> It's high treason in the amount.

After this we kept up a guard of men on the frontiers, for several months, to prevent supplies being sent to the Indians, until it was proclaimed that Sir William Johnson had made peace with them, and then we let the traders pass unmolested.

**Peace with the Indians —Sir William Johnston made peace with the Ohio Indians, Mingoes, Shawnees, and Delawares, at Johnston Hall, July 13, 1765.**

In the year 1766, I heard that Sir William Johnson, the king's agent for settling affairs with the Indians, had purchased from them all the land west of the Appalachian Mountains, that lay between the Ohio and the Cherokee River; and as I knew by conversing with the Indians in their own tongue, that there was a large body of rich land there, I concluded I would take a tour westward, and explore that country.

**Cherokee River—This is an early name for the Tennessee River which rises near the Cumberland Gap, flows southwest across Tennessee through the country of the Cherokees. It flows westward in northern Alabama, touches Mississippi, and turns north across Kentucky to join the Ohio at Paducah, Kentucky.**

I set out about the last of June, 1766, and went in the first place to Holstein River, and from thence I travelled westward in company with Joshua Horton, Uriah Stone, William Baker, and James Smith, who came from near Carlisle. There was only four white men of us, and a mulatto slave about eighteen years of age, that Mr. Horton had with him. We explored the country south of Kentucky, and there was no more sign of white men there then, than there is now west of the head waters of the Missouri. We also explored Cumberland and Tennessee Rivers, from Stone's* River down to the Ohio.

**Tennessee—This exploration by Colonel Smith and his companions was, with the single exception of that of Henry Scaggins, a hunter, the first ever made of the country west of the Cumberland mountains in Tennessee by any of the Anglo-Saxon race.**

* Stone's river is a south branch of Cumberland, and empties into it above Nashville. We first gave it this name in our journal in May 1767, after one of my fellow travellers, Mr. Uriah Stone, and I am told that it retains the same name unto this day.

When we came to the mouth of
Tennessee, my fellow travellers concluded
that they would proceeded on to the
Illinois, and see some more of the land to
the west:—this I would not agree to. As
I had already been longer from home than
what I expected, I thought my wife
would be distressed, and think
I was killed by the Indians; therefore I
concluded that I would return home.
I sent my horse with my fellow travellers
to the Illinois, as it was difficult to take a
horse through the mountains. My
comrades gave me the greatest part of
the amunition they then had, which
amounted only to half a pound of powder,
and lead equivalent. Mr. Horton also
left me his mulatto boy, and I then set
off through the wilderness, for Carolina.

About eight days after I left my
company at the mouth of Tennessee, on
my journey eastward, I got a cane stab
in my foot, which occasioned my leg to
swell, and I suffered much pain. I was
now in a doleful situation—far from
any human species, excepting black
Jamie, or the savages, and I knew not
when I might meet with them—my case
appeared desperate, and I thought
something must be done. All the surgical
instruments I had, was a knife, a
mockason awl, and a pair of bullit
moulds—with these I determined to draw
the snag from my foot, if possible. I
stuck the awl in the skin, and with the
knife I cut the flesh away from around
the cane, and then I commanded the
mulatto fellow to catch it with the
bullit moulds, and pull it out, which he

Mockason awl — Part of
the equipment of fron-
tier woodsmen, Indians,
and many soldiers was
a metal awl—a short,
pointed tool which looked
like a large needle with a
wooden handle. It was
used to make holes in
leather or buckskin to
repair moccasins, leg-
gings, or any leather ar-
ticles.

Joseph Doddridge commented that the awl was "an appendage of every shot pouch strap, together with a roll of buckskin for mending the moccasins. This was the labor of almost every evening. They were sewed together and patched with deer skin thongs, or whangs as they were commonly called."

Fodder-house—This was used as a shelter for farm animals. A crude but effective shelter was constructed by covering a framework of poles with layers of cornstalks— that is fodder—to keep out the rain, snow, and wind.

did. When I saw it, it seemed a shocking thing to be in any person's foot; it will therefore be supposed that I was very glad to have it out. The black fellow attended upon me, and obeyed my directions faithfully. I ordered him to search for Indian medicine, and told him to get me a quantity of bark from the root of a lynn tree, which I made him beat on a stone, with a tomahawk, and boil it in a kettle, and with the ooze I bathed my foot and leg:—what remained when I had finished bathing, I boiled to a jelly, and made poultices thereof. As I had no rags, I made use of the green moss that grows upon logs, and wrapped it round with elm bark: by this means (simple as it may seem) the swelling and inflamation in a great measure abated. As stormy weather appeared, I ordered Jamie to make us a shelter, which he did by erecting forks and poles, and covering them over with cane tops, like a fodder-house. It was about one hundred yards from a large buffaloe road. As we were almost out of provision, I commanded Jamie to take my gun, and I went along as well as I could, concealed myself near the road, and killed a buffaloe. When this was done, we jirked* the lean, and fryed the tallow out of the fat meat, which we kept to stew with our jirk as we needed it.

While I lay at this place, all the books I had to read was a Psalm Book, and

* Jirk is a name well known by the hunters and frontier inhabitants, for meat cut in small pieces and laid on a scaffold, over a slow fire, whereby it is roasted till it is thoroughly dry.

Watts upon Prayer. Whilst in this situation
I composed the following verses, which I
then frequently sung.

    1.   Six weeks I've in this desart been,
          With one mulatto lad,
          Excepting this poor stupid slave,
          No company I had.
    2.   In solitude I here remain,
          A cripple very sore,
          No friend or neighbor to be found,
          My case for to deplore.
    3.   I'm far from home, far from the wife,
          Which in my bosom lay,
          Far from the children dear, which
          used
          Around me for to play.
    4.   This doleful circumstance cannot
          My happiness prevent,
          While peace of conscience I enjoy,
          Great comfort and content.

    I continued in this place until I could
walk slowly, without crutches. As I now
lay near a great buffaloe road, I was
afraid that the Indians might be passing
that way, and discover my fire-place,
therefore I moved off some distance,
where I remained until I killed an elk.
As my foot was yet sore, I concluded
that I would stay here until it was healed,
least by travelling too soon, it might
again be inflamed.

    In a few weeks after, I proceeded on,
and in October I arrived in Carolina. I
had now been eleven months in the
wilderness, and during this time, I neither
saw bread, money, women, or spirituous
liquors; and three months of which I

saw none of the human species, except
Jamie.

When I came into the settlement, my
clothes were almost worn out, and the boy
had nothing on him that ever was spun.
He had buck-skin leggins, mockasons, and
breech-clout—a bear-skin dressed with
the hair on, which he belted about him,
and a racoon-skin cap. I had not
travelled far after I came in before I
was strictly examined by the inhabitants.
I told them the truth, and where I came
from, &c. but my story appeared so
strange to them, that they did not believe
me. They said they had never heard of
any one coming through the mountains
from the mouth of Tennessee; and if any
one would undertake such a journey,
surely no man would lend him his slave.
They said that they thought that all I
had told them were lies, and on suspicion
they took me into custody, and set a
guard over me.

While I was confined here, I met with
a reputable old acquaintance, who
voluntarily became my voucher; and
also told me of a number of my
acquaintances that now lived near this
place, who had moved from Pennsylvania
—On this being made public, I was
liberated. I went to a magistrate, and
obtained a pass, and one of my old
acquaintances made me a present of a
shirt. I then cast away my old rags, and
all the clothes I now had was an old
beaver hat, buck-skin leggins, mockasons,
and a new shirt; also an old blanket,
which I commonly carried on my back in
good weather. Being thus equipped, I

marched on, with my white shirt loose,
and Jamie with his bear-skin about him:—
myself appearing white, and Jamie
very black, alarmed the dogs where-ever
we came, so that they barked violently.
The people frequently came out, and
asked me where we came from, &c. I
told them the truth, but they, for the
most part suspected my story, and I
generally had to shew them my pass.
In this way I came on to Fort Chissel,
where I left Jamie at Mr. Horton's
negro-quarter, according to promise.
I went from thence to Mr. George
Adams's, on Reed Creek, where I had
lodged, and where I had left my clothes
as I was going out from home. When I
dressed myself in good clothes, and
mounted on horseback, no man ever asked
me for a pass; therefore I concluded
that a horse-thief, or even a robber,
might pass without interruption, provided
he was only well dressed, whereas the
shabby villain would be immediately
detected.

    I returned home to Conococheague,
in the fall of 1767. When I arrived, I
found that my wife and friends had
despaired of ever seeing me again, as they
had heard that I was killed by the Indians,
and my horse brought into one of the
Cherokee towns.

    In the year 1769, the Indians again
made incursions on the frontiers; yet the
traders continued carrying goods and
warlike stores to them. The frontiers took
the alarm, and a number of persons,
collected, destroyed and plundered
a quantity of their powder, lead, &c. in

**Fort Chissel** — *Fort Chis-well was built by Colonel Byrd and his regiment from Virginia in 1758; he stationed a garrison in it. . . . It stood about nine miles east of the present town of Wytheville in Wythe county.*

**Indians and Traders**—*Letters in the* Pennsylvania Gazette, *from Fort Pitt, dated July 26 and 28, 1769, mention the great probability of another war; "the Indians are so insolent, robbing houses, stealing horses, and threatening the inhabitants."*

**Traders' goods destroyed** —*Captain Robert Callender was the principal sufferer by the destruction of traders' goods at the crossings of the Juniata in Bedford county in August, 1769. He afterward applied to the legislature for relief, stating his losses at near £600.*

Bedford county. Shortly after this,
some of these persons, with others,
were apprehended and laid in irons in
the guard-house in Fort Bedford, on
suspicion of being the perpetrators of
this crime.

Though I did not altogether approve of
the conduct of this new club of black-
boys, yet I concluded that they should
not lie in irons in the guard-house, or
remain in confinement, by arbitrary
or military power. I resolved therefore,
if possible, to release them, if they even
should be tried by the civil law
afterwards. I collected eighteen of my
old black-boys, that I had seen tried in
the Indian war, &c. I did not desire a large
party, lest they should be too much
alarmed at Bedford, and accordingly
prepare for us. We marched along the
public road in day-light, and made no
secret of our design:—We told those
whom we met, that we were going to take
Fort Bedford, which appeared to them
a very unlikely story. Before this I made
it known to one William Thompson, a
man whom I could trust, and who lived
there: him I employed as a spy, and sent
him along on horse-back, before, with
orders to meet me at a certain place
near Bedford, one hour before day.
The next day a little before sun-set, we
encamped near the crossings of Juniata,
about fourteen miles from Bedford,
and erected tents, as though we intended
staying all night, and not a man in my
company knew to the contrary, save
myself. Knowing that they would hear
this in Bedford, and wishing it to be

the case, I thought to surprize them, by
stealing a march.

As the moon rose about eleven o'clock,
I ordered my boys to march, and we
went on at the rate of five miles an hour,
until we met Thompson at the place
appointed. He told us that the
commanding officer had frequently heard
of us by travellers, and had ordered
thirty men upon guard. He said they
knew our number, and only made game
of the notion of eighteen men coming to
rescue the prisoners, but they did not
expect us until towards the middle of the
day. I asked him if the gate was open?
He said it was then shut, but he expected
they would open it as usual, at day-
light, as they apprehended no danger.
I then moved my men privately up under
the banks of Juniata, where we lay
concealed about one hundred yards from
the fort gate. I had ordered the men to
keep a profound silence, until we got into
it. I then sent off Thompson again, to spy.
At day-light he returned, and told us that
the gate was open, and three centinels
were standing on the wall—that the
guards were taking a morning dram,
and the arms standing together in one
place. I then concluded to rush into the
fort, and told Thompson to run before
me to the arms. We ran with all our might,
and as it was a misty morning, the
centinels scarcely saw us until we were
within the gate, and took possession of the
arms. Just as we were entering, two of
them discharged their guns, though I do
not believe they aimed at us. We then
raised a shout, which surprized the

Affray near Bedford— *Smith was committed to the jail in Carlisle on the 22d of September, 1769, charged with shooting John Johnston on the 20th of the same month. A large body of armed men assembled to rescue him fearing (they said) he would be taken to Philadelphia for trial. Col. John Armstrong, the Rev. John Steel, and other leading citizens, endeavored to dissuade them from their purpose, while the magistrates assisted the sheriff in raising a guard to defend the jail. Smith sent his intended rescuers "a candid letter declaring his desire to have a trial by the laws of his country, begging them to return home," etc. They did not desist, however, until from the windows of the prison he "begged them in a solemn manner to return, and to shed no innocent blood;" this, with assurances that the prisoner should be tried in the county and not elsewhere, turned them reluctantly from their design.*

Snapped a pistol—*Smith's assailant, Robert George, attempted to shoot him but the priming charge in the pan of his flintlock pistol failed to ignite when the hammer fell. The pistol misfired, or "snapped," a common malfunction with flintlock guns.*

My gun blowed or made a slow fire—*Sometimes the priming charge in the pan of a flintlock rifle failed to ignite the main powder charge in the barrel immediately, result-*

town, though some of them were well pleased with the news. We compelled a black-smith to take the irons off the prisoners, and then we left the place. This, I believe, was the first British fort in America, that was taken by what they called American rebels.

Some time after this I took a journey west ward, in order to survey some located land I had on and near the Youhogany. As I passed near Bedford, while I was walking and leading my horse, I was overtaken by some men on horse-back, like travellers. One of them asked my name, and on telling it, they immediately pulled out their pistols, and presented them at me, calling upon me to deliver myself, or I was a dead man. I stepped back, presented my rifle, and told them to stand off. One of them snapped a pistol at me, and another was preparing to shoot, when I fired my piece: —one of them also fired near the same time, and one of my fellow travellers fell. The assailants then rushed up, and as my gun was empty, they took and tied me. I charged them with killing my fellow traveller, and told them he was a man that I had accidentally met with on the road, that had nothing to do with the public quarrel. They asserted that I had killed him. I told them that my gun blowed, or made a slow fire—that I had her from my face before she went off, or I would not have missed my mark; and from the position my piece was in when it went off, it was not likely that my gun killed this man, yet I acknowledged I was not certain that it was not so. They

then carried me to Bedford, laid me in
irons in the guard-house, summed a jury
of the opposite party, and held an
inquest. The jury brought me in guilty of
wilful murder. As they were afraid to keep
me long in Bedford, for fear of a rescue,
they sent me privately through the
wilderness to Carlisle, where I was
laid in heavy irons.

Shortly after I came here, we heard that
a number of my old black boys were
coming to tear down the jail. I told the
sheriff that I would not be rescued, as I
knew that the indictment was wrong;
therefore I wished to stand my trial. As
I had found the black boys to be always
under good command, I expected I could
prevail on them to return, and therefore
wished to write to them—to this the
sheriff readily agreed. I wrote a letter to
them, with irons on my hands, which was
immediately sent; but as they had heard
that I was in irons, they would come on.
When we heard they were near the town,
I told the sheriff I would speak to them
out of the window, and if the irons were
off, I made no doubt but I could prevail
on them to desist. The sheriff ordered
them to be taken off, and just as they were
taken off my hands, the black boys came
running up to the jail. I went to the
window and called to them, and they gave
attention. I told them as my indictment
was for wilful murder, to admit of being
rescued, would appear dishonorable. I
thanked them for their kind intentions,
and told them the greatest favor they
could confer upon me, would be to grant
me this one request, <u>to withdraw from</u>

ing in a "slow fire" or
"hang fire," and a lapse
of several seconds or more
before the firearm dis-
charged. This was some-
times described as "long
fired."

the jail, and return in peace: to this they
complied, and withdrew. While I was
speaking, the irons were taken off my
feet, and never again put on.

Before this party arrived at
Conococheague, they met above three
hundred more, on the way, coming to
their assistance, and were resolved to
take me out; they then turned, and all
came together, to Carlisle. The reason
they gave for coming again, was, because
they thought that government was so
enraged at me that I would not get a fair
trial; but my friends and myself together,
again prevailed on them to return in
peace.

At this time the public papers were
partly filled with these occurrences. The
following is an extract from the
Pennsylvania Gazette, number 2132,
November 2d, 1769.

"Conococheague, October 16th, 1769.

"MESS. HALL & SELLERS,

"Please to give the following narrative a
place in your Gazette, and you will much
oblige

"Your humble servant,

"WILLIAM SMITH."

"Whereas, in this Gazette of September
28th, 1769, there appeared an extract of a
letter from Bedford, September 12th, 1769,
relative to James Smith, as being apprehended
on suspicion of being a black boy, then
killing his companion, &c. I took upon myself
as bound by all the obligations of truth,
justice to character and to the world, to set

that matter in a true light; by which, I hope
the impartial world will be enabled to obtain
a more just opinion of the present scheme of
acting in this end of the country, as also
to form a true idea of the truth, candor,
and ingenuity of the author of the said
extract, in stating that matter in so partial
a light. The state of the case (which can be
made appear by undeniable evidence,) was
this: James Smith, (who is styled the
principal ring leader of the black boys,
by the said author) together with his younger
brother, and brother-in-law, were going out
in order to survey and improve their land on
the waters of Youghoghany, and as the time
of their return was long, they took with them
their arms, and horses loaded with the
necessaries of life: and as one of Smith's
brothers-in-law was an artist in surveying, he
had also with him the instruments for that
business. Travelling on the way, within
about nine miles of Bedford, they overtook,
and joined company with one Johnson and
Moorhead, who likewise had horses loaded,
part of which loading was liquor, and part
seed wheat, their intentions being to make
improvements on their lands. When they
arrived at the parting of the road on this
side Bedford, the company separated, one
part going through the town, in order to get
a horse shod, were apprehended, and put
under confinement, but for what crime they
knew not, and treated in a manner utterly
inconsistent with the laws of their country,
and the liberties of Englishmen:—Whilst
the other part, viz. James Smith, Johnson,
and Moorhead, taking along the other
road, were met by John Holmes esq. to whom
James Smith spoke in a friendly manner,
but received no answer. Mr. Holmes hasted,
and gave an alarm in Bedford, from whence
a party of men were sent in pursuit of them;

but Smith and his companions not having the
least thought of any such measures being
taken, (why should they?) travelled slowly on.
After they had gained the place where the
roads joined, they delayed until the other
part of their company should come up.
At this time a number of men came riding,
like men travelling; they asked Smith
his name, which he told them—on which
they immediately assaulted him as highway-
men, and with presented pistols, commanded
him to surrender, or he was a dead man; upon
which Smith stepped back, asked them if
they were highway-men, charging them at
the same time to stand off, when immediately,
Robert George (one of the assailants)
snapped a pistol at Smith's head, and that
before Smith offered to shoot, (which
said George himself acknowledged upon
oath;) whereupon Smith presented
his gun at another of the assailants, who
was preparing to shoot him with his pistol.
The said assailant having a hold of Johnson
by the arm, two shots were fired, one by
Smith's gun, the other from a pistol, so
quick as just to be distinguishable, and
Johnson fell. After which Smith was taken
and carried into Bedford, where John
Holmes, esq. the informer, held an inquest
on the corpse, one of the assailants being
as an evidence, (nor was there any other
troubled about the matter) Smith was
brought in guilty of wilful murder, and so
committed to prison. But a jealousy arising in
the breasts of many that the inquest, either
through inadvertency, ignorance or some
other default, was not so fair as it ought to
be; William Deny, coroner of the county,
upon requisition made, thought proper to re-
examine the matter, and summoning a jury
of unexceptionable men, out of three
townships—men whose candor, probity and

honesty, is unquestionable with all who
are acquainted with them, and having raised
the corpse, held an inquest in a solemn
manner, during three days. In the course of
their scrutiny they found Johnson's shirt
blacked about the bullit-hole, by the powder
of the charge by which he was killed,
whereupon they examined into the distance
Smith stood from Johnson when he shot, and
one of the assailants being admitted to
oath, swore to the respective spots of ground
they both stood on at that time, which the
jury measured, and found to be twenty-three
feet, nearly; then trying the experiment of
shooting at the same shirt, both with and
against the wind, and at the same distance,
found no effects, nor the least stain from
the powder, on the shirt:—And let any
person that pleases, make the experiment,
and I will venture to affirm he shall find that
powder will not stain at half the distance
mentioned, if shot out of a rifle gun, which
Smith's was. Upon the whole, the jury, after
the most accurate examination, and mature
deliberation, brought in their verdict that
some one of the assailants themselves must
necessarily have been the perpetrators of the
murder.

"I have now represented the matter in its
true and genuine colors, and which I will
abide by. I only beg liberty to make a few
remarks and reflections on the above
mentioned extract. The author says "James
Smith, with two others in company, passed
round the town, without touching," by
which it is plain he would insinuate, and
make the public believe that Smith, and that
part of the company, had taken some bye-
road, which is utterly false, for it was the
king's high-way, and the straightest, that
through Bedford, being something to the
one side, nor would the other part of the

company have gone through the town, but
for the reason already given. Again, the
author says, that "four men were sent in
pursuit of Smith and his companions, who
overtook them about five miles from Bedford,
and commanded them to surrender, on which
Smith presented his gun at one of the men,
who was struggling with his companion,
fired it at him, and shot his companion
through the back." Here I would just remark
again, the unfair and partial account given of
this matter, by the author; not a word
mentioned of George's snapping his pistol
before Smith offered to shoot, or of another
of the assailants actually firing his pistol,
though he confessed himself afterwards, he
had done so; not the least mention of the
company's baggage, which, to men in the
least open to a fair enquiry, would have been
sufficient proof of the innocence of their
intentions. Must not an effusive blush
overspread the face of the partial representer
of facts, when he finds the veil he had thrown
over truth thus pulled aside, and she exposed
to naked view. Suppose it should be
granted that Smith shot the man, (which
is not, and I presume never can be proven
to be the case) I would only ask, was he not
on his own defence? Was he not publicly
assaulted? Was he not charged at the peril
of his life, to surrender, without knowing
for what? No warrant being shown him, or
any declaration made of their authority.
And seeing these things are so, would any
judicious man, any person in the least
acquainted with the laws of the land, or
morality, judge him guilty of wilful murder?
But I humbly presume every one who has an
opportunity of seeing this, will by this time
be convinced that the proceedings against
Smith were truly unlawful and tyranical,
perhaps unparalleled by any instance in a

civilized nation; for to endeavor to kill a man in the apprehending him, in order to bring him to trial for a fact, and that too on a supposed one, is undoubtedly beyond all bounds of law or government.

"If the author of the extract thinks I have treated him unfair, or that I have advanced any thing he can controvert, let him come forward as a fair antagonist, and make his defence, and I will, if called upon, vindicate all that I have advanced against him or his abettors.

                    "WILLIAM SMITH."


I remained in prison four months, and during this time I often thought of those that were confined in the time of the persecution, who declared their prison was converted into a palace. I now learned what this meant, as I never since, or before, experienced four months of equal happiness.

When the supreme court sat, I was severely prosecuted. At the commencement of my trial, the judges in a very unjust and arbitrary manner, rejected several of my evidences; yet, as Robert George (one of those who was in the fray when I was taken) swore in court that he snapped a pistol at me before I shot, and a concurrence of corroborating circumstances, amounted to strong presumptive evident that it could not possibly be my gun that killed Johnson, the jury, without hesitation, brought in their verdict, NOT GUILTY. One of the judges then declared that not one of this jury should ever hold any office above a constable.

Commissioner of Bedford and Westmoreland Counties—*Colonel Smith had removed to his land on Jacob's creek, a branch of the Youghiogheny, then in Bedford county, which was erected in 1771, and included all of the Western part of the province. From Bedford, Westmoreland county was formed in 1773; it embraced within its limits all of the province west of the Laurel Hill. This territory was claimed by Virginia, whose jurisdiction over it the governor, Lord Dunmore, attempted by violent measures to enforce. Fort Pitt was seized by a band of armed partizans, headed by Captain John Connolly, and its name changed to Fort Dunmore. New counties were formed from which delegates were sent to the Virginia legislature. Justices and other civil officers were commissioned by the authorities of Virginia. Court-houses were erected and Virginia courts regularly held within the limits of the present counties of Allegheny and Washington in Pennsylvania. The people were divided in their allegiance; arrests, counter-arrests, and other violent acts, frequently occurred during this seven years' contest. The breaking out of the Revolutionary war in 1775 and a recommendation by Congress on the subject abated the civil strife. The controversy ended in 1780 by mutual agreement between the two states, Virginia yielding her claims to the disputed territory. The completion of Mason and Dixon's line in 1784, permanently settled the boundary.*

*For three years of these turbulent times James Smith was one of the commissioners of*

Notwithstanding this proud, ill-natured declaration, some of these jurymen afterwards filled honorable places, and I myself was elected the next year, and sat on the board* in Bedford county, and afterwards I served in the board three years in Westmoreland county.

In the year 1774, another Indian war commenced, though at this time the white people were the aggressors. The prospect of this terrified the frontier inhabitants, insomuch that the great part on the Ohio waters, either fled over the mountains, eastward, or collected into forts. As the state of Pennsylvania apprehended great danger, they at this time appointed me captain over what was then called the Pennsylvania line. As they knew I could raise men that would answer their purpose, they seemed to lay aside their former inveteracy.

In the year 1776, I was appointed a major in the Pennsylvania association. When American independence was declared, I was elected a member of the convention in Westmoreland county, state of Pennsylvania, and of the assembly as long as I proposed to serve.

While I attended the assembly in Philadelphia, in the year 1777, I saw in the street, some of my old boys, on their way to the Jerseys, against the British, and they desired me to go with them—

* A board of commissioners was annually elected in Pennsylvania, to regulate taxes, and lay the county levy.

I petitioned the house for leave of absence, in order to head a scouting party, which was granted me. We marched into the Jerseys, and went before General Washington's army, way-laid the road at Rocky Hill, attacked about two hundred of the British, and with thirty-six men drove them out of the woods into a large open field. After this, we attacked a party that were guarding the officers baggage, and took the waggon and twenty two Hessians; and also re-took some of our continental soldiers which they had with them. In a few days we killed and took more of the British, than was of our party. At this time I took the camp fever, and was carried in a stage waggon to Burlington, where I lay until I recovered. When I took sick, my companion, Major James M'Common, took the command of the party, and had greater success than I had. If every officer and his party that lifted arms against the English, had fought with the same success that Major M'Common did, we would have made short work of the British war.

When I returned to Philadelphia, I applied to the assembly for leave to raise a battallion of riflemen, which they appeared very willing to grant, but said they could not do it, as the power of raising men and commissioning officers was at that time committed to General Washington, therefore they advised me to apply to his excellency. The following is a true copy of a letter of recommendation which I received at this time, from the council of safety:

Hessians—German mercenaries serving the British during the American Revolution.

Camp fever—Typhus, or prison-fever, was a virulent, contagious fever sometimes transmitted by lice.

Council of Safety—This council, or Committee of Safety, was an official body empowered to investigate suspected loyalists, to obtain military supplies, etc.

## "IN COUNCIL OF SAFETY,

"Philadelphia, February 10th, 1777.

"Sir—Application has been made to us by James Smith esq. of Westmoreland, a gentleman well acquainted with the Indian customs, and their manner of carrying on war, for leave to raise a battallion of marksmen, expert in the use of rifles, and such as are acquainted with the Indian method of fighting, to be dressed entirely in their fashion, for the purpose of annoying and harrassing the enemy in their marches and encampments. We think two or three hundred men in that way, might be very useful. Should your excellency be of the same opinion, and direct such a corps to be formed, we will take proper measures for raising the men on the frontiers of this state, and follow such other directions as your excellency shall give in this manner.

"To his excellency, General Washington."

"The foregoing is a copy of a letter to his excellency, General Washington, from the council of safety.

"JACOB S. HOWELL, Secretary,"

After this I received another letter of recommendation, which is as follows:

"We whose names are under written, do certify that James Smith, (now of the county of Westmoreland) was taken prisoner by the Indians, in an expedition before General Braddock's defeat, in the year 1755, and remained with them until the year 1760: and also that he served as ensign, in the year 1763, under the pay of the province of Pennsylvania, and as lieutenant, in the year 1764, and as captain, in the year 1774; and as

a military officer, he has sustained a good
character:—And we do recommend him
as a person well acquainted with the Indian's
method of fighting, and, in our humble
opinion, exceedingly fit for the command of
a ranging or scouting party, which we are
also humbly of opinion, he could (if legally
authorized) soon raise. Given under our
hands at Philadelphia, this 13th day of
March, 1777.

| | |
|---|---|
| Thomas Paxton, capt. | Jonathan Hoge, esq. |
| William Duffield, esq. | William Parker, capt. |
| David Robb, esq. | Robert Elliot, |
| John Piper, col. | Joseph Armstrong, col. |
| William M'Comb, | |
| William Pepper, lieut. col. | Robert Peebles, lieut. col. |
| James M'Clane, esq. | Samuel Patton, capt. |
| John Proctor, col. | William Lyon, esq. |

With these, and some other letters of
recommendation, which I have not now in
my possession, I went to his excellency,
who lay at Morristown. Though General
Washington did not fall in with the
scheme of white-men turning Indians,
yet he proposed giving me a major's
place in a battallion of rifle men already
raised. I thanked the general for his
proposal; but as I entertained no high
opinion of the colonel that I was to serve
under, and with him I had no prospect
of getting my old boys again, I thought
I would be of more use in the cause we
were then struggling to support, to remain
with them as a militia officer, therefore
I did not accept this offer.
    In the year 1778, I received a colonel's

**Indians' Attack**—*The date of the year in the narrative is erroneous, it should be 1777. [Arch Lockry wrote] "I have sent five Indian scalps taken by one of our scouting party, commanded by Colonel Barr, Colonel Perry, Colonel Smith, and Captain Hinkston, being volunteers in the action. The action happened near Kittaning, they retook six horses the savages had taken from the suffering frontiers."*

**Took four scalps**—Some Indian fighters and frontiersmen scalped or mutilated fallen enemies just as the Indians did, perhaps, as a gesture of defiance or retaliation. Little respect for enemy dead was shown by either Indians or whites. Often the bodies of those who fell in battle were subjected to shocking mutilation. Grisly trophies made from human skin were sometimes carried by frontier riflemen or Indian warriors. Even women and children did not escape the scalping knife. Daniel Boone seems to be one noted frontier fighter who did not take scalps.

**French Creek Expedition**
MINUTES OF THE SUPREME EXECUTIVE COUNCIL,
Philadephia,
March 20, 1786.

*Comptroller General's reports upon the following accounts read and approved, viz: Of Captain John Woods for pay of his company of Westmoreland county militia, commanded by Colonel Smith under orders from General McIntosh, and for arms lost on the expedition.*

commission, and after my return to Westmoreland, the indians made an attack upon our frontiers. I then raised men and pursued them, and the second day we overtook and defeated them. We likewise took four scalps, and recovered the horses and plunder which they were carrying off. At the time of this attack, Captain John Hinkston pursued an Indian, both their guns being empty, and after the fray was over he was missing:—While we were enquiring about him, he came walking up, seemingly unconcerned, with a bloody scalp in his hand—he had pursued the Indian about a quarter of a mile, and tomahawked him.

Not long after this I was called upon to command four hundred riflemen, on an expedition against the Indian town on French Creek. It was some time in November, before I received orders from General M'Intosh, to march, and then we were poorly equipped, and scarce of provisions. We marched in three columns, forty rod from each other. There were also flankers on the outside of each column, that marched a-breast, in the rear, in scattered order—and even in the columns, the men were one rod apart—and in the front, the volunteers marched a-breast, in the same manner of the flankers, scouring the woods. In case of an attack, the officers were immediately to order the men to face out and take trees—in this position the Indians could not avail themselves by surrounding us, or have an opportunity of shooting a man from either side of the tree. If attacked, the centre column was to reinforce whatever part appeared to require it most. When we encamped, our encampment formed a hollow square, including about thirty or forty acres—on the outside of the square there were centinels placed, whose business it was to watch for the enemy, and see that neither horses or bullocks went out:—And when encamped, if any attacks were made by an enemy, each officer was immediately to order the men to face out and take trees, as before mentioned; and in this form they could not take the advantage by surrounding us, as they commonly had done when they fought the whites.

The following is a copy of general orders, given at this time, which I have found among my journals:

## "AT CAMP—OPPOSITE FORT PITT,

### November 29th, 1778.

### "GENERAL ORDERS:

#### "A copy thereof is to be given to each captain and subaltern, and to be read to each company.

"You are to march in three columns, with flankers on the front and rear, and to keep a profound silence, and not to fire a gun, except at the enemy, without particular orders for that purpose; and in case of an attack, let it be so ordered that every other man only, is to shoot at once, excepting on extraordinary occasions. The one half of the men to keep a reserve fire, until their comrades load; and let every one be particularly careful not to fire at any time, without a view of the enemy, and that not at too great a distance. I earnestly urge the above caution, as I have

*Of Captain John Kyle, for pay of his company employed on the said expedition.*

*Of Colonel James Smith, for pay of the militia of Westmoreland county, under his command, employed on the French creek expedition in 1778.*

General McIntosh—*Brigadier General Lachlan McIntosh of the Continental army succeeded General Hand in command of the Western district; (head quarters at Fort Pitt) in May, 1778. In October following he built Fort McIntosh, "upon the Indian side of the Ohio river" (where the town of Beaver now stands), and in November and December erected Fort Laurens on the west bank of the Tuscarawas river, half a mile below the present town of Bolivar, Tuscarawas county, Ohio.*

Journals—Smith was able to keep a journal during his captivity, which was unusual. When he put his story into book form his notes were a great asset, for most captivity narratives were written years later from memory. Apparently Smith continued to keep journals all his life. Some of these may still survive, and if they are found would be of rare historical value.

known very remarkable and grievous errors
of this kind. You are to encamp on the hollow
square, except the volunteers, who,
according to their own request, are to
encamp on the front of the square. A sufficient
number of centinels are to be kept round the
square, at a proper distance. Every man is to
be under arms at the break of day, and to
parade opposite to their fire-places, facing
out, and when the officers examine their
arms, and find them in good order, and give
necessary directions, they are to be dismissed,
with orders to have their arms near them,
and be always in readiness.

"Given by

"JAMES SMITH, <u>Colonel</u>."


In this manner we proceeded on, to
French Creek, where we found the
Indian town evacuated. I then went on
further than my orders called for, in quest
of Indians; but our provisions being
nearly exhausted, we were obliged to
return. On our way back, we met with
considerable difficulties, on account of
high waters and scarcity of provision;
yet we never lost one horse, excepting
some that gave out.

After peace was made with the Indians,
I met with some of them in Pittsburg,
and enquired of them in their own
tongue, concerning this expedition,—
not letting them know I was there. They
told me that they watched the movements
of this army ever after they had left
Fort-Pitt, and as they passed thro the
glades or barrens they had a full view
of them from the adjacent hills and

computed their number to be about one
thousand. They said they also examined
their camps, both before and after they
were gone, and found, they could not
make an advantageous attack, and
therefore moved off from their town and
hunting ground before we arrived.

In the year 1788 I settled in Bourbon
county, Kentucky, seven miles above
Paris; and in the same year was elected
a member of the convention, that sat at
Danville, to confer about a separation
from the state of Virginia.—and from
that year until the year 1799, I represented
Bourbon county, either in convention or
as a member of the general assembly,
except two years that I was left a few
votes behind.


# ON THE MANNERS AND
# CUSTOMS OF THE INDIANS.


The Indians are a slovenly people in
their dress.—They seldom ever wash
their shirts, and in regard to cookery
they are exceedingly filthy. When they
kill a buffaloe they will sometimes lash
the paunch of it round a sapling, and
cast it into the kettle, boil it and sup the
broth; tho they commonly shake it
about in cold water, then boil and eat it.—
Notwithstanding all this, they are
very polite in their own way, and they

Illustration of Colonel James Smith adapted from an oil painting said to have been painted by Chester Harding. Used with the permission of portrait owner Warren Shonert who lives in Falmouth, Kentucky.

retain among them the essentials of good
manners; tho they have few compliments,
yet they are complaisant to one another,
and when accompanied with good
humour and discretion, they entertain
strangers in the best manner their
circumstances will admit. They use but
few titles of honor. In the military line,
the titles of great men are only captains
or leaders of parties—In the civil
line, the titles are only councilors, chiefs
or the old wisemen. These titles are never
made use of in addressing any of their
great men. The language commonly made
use of in addressing them is, Grandfather,
Father, or Uncle. They have no such thing
in use among them as Sir, Mr. Madam
or Mistress—The common mode of
address, is, my Friend, Brother, Cousin,
or Mother Sister, &c. They pay great
respect to age; or to the aged Fathers
and Mothers among them of every rank.
No one can arrive at any place of honor,
among them, but by merit. Either some
exploit in war, must be performed, before
any one can be advanced in the military
line, or become eminent for wisdom
before they can obtain a seat in council.
It would appear to the Indians a most
ridiculous thing to see a man lead
off a company of warriors, as an officer,
who had himself never been in a battle
in his life: even in case of merit, they are
slow in advancing any one, until they
arrive at or near middle-age.

They invite every one that comes to
their house, or camp to eat, while they
have any thing to give; and it is accounted
bad manners to refuse eating, when

invited. They are very tenacious of their
old mode of dressing and painting, and do
not change their fashions as we do. They
are very fond of tobacco, and the men
almost all smoke it mixed with sumach
leaves or red willow bark, pulverized,
tho they seldom use it in any other way.
They make use of the pipe also as a token
of love and friendship.

In courtship they also differ from us.
It is a common thing among them for a
young woman, if in love, to make suit to
a young man: tho the first address may be
by the man; yet the other is the most
common. The squaws are generally very
immodest in their words and actions,
and will often put the young men to the
blush. The men commonly appear to be
possessed of much more modesty than
the women; yet I have been acquainted
with some young squaws that appeared
really modest: genuine it must be, as
they were under very little restraint in the
channel of education or custom.

When the Indians meet one-another,
instead of saying, how do you do, they
commonly salute in the following manner
—you are my friend—the reply is, truly
friend, I am your friend,—or, cousin, you
yet exist—the reply is certainly I do.
They have their children under tolerable
command: seldom ever whip them, and
their common mode of chastising, is by
ducking them in cold water; therefore
their children are more obedient in the
winter season, than they are in the
summer; tho they are then not so often
ducked. They are a peaceable people, and
scarcely ever wrangle or scold, when sober;

but they are very much addicted to
drinking, and men and women will
become basely intoxicated, if they can,
by any means, procure or obtain
spirituous liquor; and then they are
commonly either extremely merry and
kind, or very turbulent, ill-humoured
and disorderly.

## ON THEIR TRADITIONS AND RELIGIOUS SENTIMENTS.

As the family that I was adopted
into was intermarried with the Wiandots
and Ottawas, three tongues were
commonly spoke, viz. Caughnewaga, or
what the French call Iroque, also the
Wiandot and Ottawa; by this means I
had an opportunity of learning these
three tongues; and I found that these
nations varied in their traditions and
opinions concerning religion;—and
even numbers of the same nation differed
widely in their religious sentiments.
Their traditions are vague, whimsical,
romantic and many of them scarce
worth relating; and not any of them reach
back to the creation of the world. The
Wiandots comes the nearest to this. They
tell of a squaw that was found when an
infant, in the water in a canoe made of
bull rushes: this squaw became a great
prophetress and did many wonderful
things; she turned water into dry land,
and at length made this continent, which
was, at that time, only a very small island,
and but a few Indians in it. Tho they were

then but few they had not sufficient room to hunt; therefore this squaw went to the water side, and prayed that this little island might be enlarged. The great being then heard her prayer, and sent great numbers of Water Tortoises, and Musk rats, which brought with them mud and other materials, for enlarging this island, and by this means, they say, it was increased to the size that it now remains; therefore they say, that the white people ought not to encroach upon them, or take their land from them, because their great grand mother made it.—They say, that about this time the angels or heavenly inhabitants, as they call them, frequently visited them and talked with their forefathers; and gave directions how to pray, and how to appease the great being when he was offended. They told them they were to offer sacrifice, burn tobacco, buffaloe and deer bones; but they were not to burn bears or raccoons bones, in sacrifice.

The Ottawas say, that there are two great beings that rule and govern the universe, who are at war with each other; the one they call <u>Maneto</u>, and the other <u>Matchemaneto</u>. They say that Maneto is all kindness and love, and that Matchemaneto is an evil spirit, that delights in doing mischief; and some of them think, that they are equal in power, and therefore worship the evil spirit out of a principle of fear. Others doubt which of the two may be the most powerful, and therefore endeavor to keep in favor with both, by giving each of them some kind of worship. Others say

that Maneto is the first great cause and
therefore must be all powerful and
supreme, and ought to be adored and
worshipped; whereas Matchemaneto
ought to be rejected and dispised.

Those of the Ottawas that worship the
evil spirit, pretend to be great conjurors.
I think if there is any such thing now in
the world as witchcraft, it is among these
people. I have been told wonderful
stories concerning their proceedings; but
never was eye witness to any thing that
appeared evidently supernatural.

Some of the Wiandots and
Caughnewagas profess to be Roman-
catholics; but even these retain many
of the notions of their ancestors. Those
of them who reject the Roman-catholic
religion, hold that there is one great
first cause, whom they call Owaneeyo,
that rules and governs the universe, and
takes care of all his creatures, rational
and irrational, and gives them their food
in due season, and hears the prayers of
all those that call upon him; therefore it
is but just and reasonable to pray, and
offer sacrifice to this great being, and to
do those things that are pleasing in his
sight;—but they differ widely in what is
pleasing or displeasing to this great being.
Some hold that following nature of their
own propensities is the way to happiness,
and cannot be displeasing to the deity,
because he delights in the happiness of
his creatures, and does nothing in vain;
but gave these dispositions with a design
to lead to happiness, and therefore they
ought to be followed. Others reject this
opinion altogether, and say that following

their own propensities in this manner, is
neither the means of happiness nor the
way to please the deity.

Tecaughretanego was of opinion that
following nature in a limited sense was
reasonable and right. He said that most
of the irrational animals by following their
natural propensities, were led to the
greatest pitch of happiness that their
natures and the world they lived in would
admit of. He said that mankind and the
rattle snakes had evil dispositions, that
led them to injure themselves and others.
He gave instances of this. He said he had
a puppy that he did not intend to raise,
and in order to try an experiment, he tyed
this puppy on a pole and held it to a
rattle snake, which bit it several times;
that he observed the snake shortly after,
rolling about apparently in great misery,
so that it appeared to have poisoned itself
as well as the puppy. The other instance
he gave was concerning himself. He said
that when he was a young man, he was
very fond of the women, and at length got
the venereal disease, so that by following
this propensity, he was led to injure
himself and others. He said our happiness
depends on our using our reason in order
to suppress these evil dispositions;
but when our propensities neither lead
us to injure ourselves nor others, we
might with safety indulge them, or even
pursue them as the means of happiness.

The Indians generally, are of opinion
that there are great numbers of inferior
Deities, which they call Carreyagaroona,
which signifies the Heavenly Inhabitants.
These beings they suppose are employed

Venereal disease — Several authors have commented ironically about the frontiersmen's gifts to the Indians: venereal disease, alcohol, and gunpowder.

as assistants, in managing the affairs of
the universe, and in inspecting the
actions of men: and that even the
irrational animals are engaged in viewing
their actions, and bearing intelligence
to the Gods. The eagle, for this purpose,
with her keen eye, is soaring about in the
day, and the owl, with her nightly eye,
perched on the trees around their camp
in the night; therefore, when they observe
the eagle or the owl near, they
immediately offer sacrifice, or burn
tobacco, that they may have a good report
to carry to the Gods. They say that there
are also great numbers of evil spirits,
which they call <u>Onasahroona</u>, which
signifies the Inhabitants of the Lower
Region. These they say are employed
in disturbing the world, and the good
spirits are always going after them,
and setting things right, so that they are
constantly working in opposition to each
other. Some talk of a future state, but
not with any certainty: at best their
notions are vague and unsettled. Others
deny a future state altogether, and say
that after death they neither think or live.

As the Caugnewagas and the six
nations speak nearly the same language,
their theology is also nearly alike. When
I met with the Shawanees or Delawares,
as I could not speak their tongue, I
spoke Ottawa to them, and as it bore
some resemblance to their language, we
understood each other in some common
affairs, but as I could only converse with
them very imperfectly, I cannot from my
own knowledge, with certainty, give any
account of their theological opinions.

Six Nations — The Iro-
quois confederacy was
composed of the Cayuga,
Mohawk, Oneida, Onon-
daga, Seneca, and Tus-
carora tribes.

## ON THEIR POLICE, OR CIVIL GOVERNMENT.

I have often heard of Indian Kings, but never saw any.—How any term used by the Indians in their own tongue, for the chief man of a nation, could be rendered King, I know not. The chief of a nation is neither a supreme ruler, monarch or potentate—He can neither make war or peace, leagues or treaties— He cannot impress soldiers, or dispose of magazines—He cannot adjourn, prorogue or dissolve a general assembly, nor can he refuse his assent to their conclusions, or in any manner controul them—With them there is no such thing as hereditary succession, title of nobility or royal blood, even talked of.—The chief of a nation, even with the consent of his assembly, or council, cannot raise one shilling of tax off the citizens, but only receive what they please to give as free and voluntary donations—The chief of a nation has to hunt for his living, as any other citizen— How then can they with any propriety, be called kings? I apprehend that the white people were formerly so fond of the name of kings, and so ignorant of their power, that they concluded the chief man of a nation must be a king.

As they are illiterate, they consequently have no written code of laws. What they execute as laws, are either old customs, or the immediate result of new councils. Some of their ancient laws or customs are very pernicious, and disturb the public weal. Their vague law of marriage

Public weal — This refers to the well-being or prosperity of the community.

is a glaring instance of this, as the
man and his wife are under no legal
obligation to live together, if they are
both willing to part. They have little
form, or ceremony among them, in
matrimony, but do like the Israelites
of old—the man goes in unto the woman
and she becomes his wife. The years of
puberty and the age of consent, is about
fourteen for the woman, and eighteen
for the men. Before I was taken by the
Indians, I had often heard that in the
ceremony of marriage, the man gave the
woman a deer's leg, and she gave him a
red ear of corn, signifying that she was
to keep him in bread, and he was to keep
her in meat. I enquired of them
concerning the truth of this, and they
said they knew nothing of it, further than
that they had heard it was an ancient
custom among some nations. Their
frequent changing of partners prevents
propagation, creates disturbances,
and often occasions murder and
bloodshed; though this is commonly
committed under the pretence of being
drunk. Their impunity to crimes
committed when intoxicated with
spirituous liquors, or their admitting
one crime as an excuse for another, is a
very unjust law or custom.

The extremes they run into in dividing
the nececessaries of life, are hurtful to
the public weal; though their dividing
meat when hunting, may answer a
valuable purpose, as one family may have
success one day, and the other the next;
but their carrying this custom to the
town, or to agriculture, is striking at

the root of industry, as industrious persons ought to be rewarded, and the lazy suffer for their indolence.

They have scarcely any penal laws: the principal punishment is degrading: even murder is not punished by any formal law, only the friends of the murdered are at liberty to slay the murderer, if some attonement is not made. Their not annexing penalties to their laws, is perhaps not as great a crime, or as unjust and cruel, as the bloody laws of England, which we have so long shamefully practised, and which are to be in force in this state, until our penitentiary house is finished, which is now building, and then they are to be repealed.

Bloody laws of England —Smith is probably referring to the severe punishments mandated by British laws. The penalties for even minor offenses were often extreme. Those found guilty might be branded; whipped; hanged, drawn and quartered; have their ears cut off; or be subjected to other cruel and unusual punishments.

Let us also take a view of the advantages attending Indian police:— They are not oppressed or perplexed with expensive litigation—They are not injured by legal robbery—They have no splendid villains that make themselves grand and great upon other peoples labor—They have neither church nor state erected as money-making machines.

## ON THEIR DISCIPLINE, AND METHOD OF WAR.

I have often heard the British officers call the Indians the undisciplined savages, which is a capital mistake—as they have all the essentials of discipline. They are under good command, and

punctual in obeying orders: they can act
in concert, and when their officers lay a
plan and give orders, they will chearfully
unite in putting all their directions into
immediate execution; and by each man
observing the motion or movement of his
right hand companion, they can
communicate the motion from right to
left, and march a-breast in concert, and in
scattered order, though the line may be
more than a mile long, and continue,
if occasion requires, for a considerable
distance, without disorder or confusion.
They can perform various necessary
manoeuvres, either slowly, or as fast as
they can run: they can form a circle, or
semi-circle: the circle they make use of,
in order to surround their enemy, and the
semi-circle, if the enemy has a river on
one side of them. They can also form a
large hollow square, face out and
take trees: this they do, if their enemies
are about surrounding them, to prevent
being shot from either side of the tree.
When they go into battle they are not
loaded or encumbered with many
clothes, as they commonly fight naked,
save only breech-clout, leggins and
mockesons. There is no such thing as
corporeal punishment used, in order to
bring them under such good discipline:
degrading is the only chastisement, and
they are so unanimous in this, that it
effectually answers the purpose. Their
officers plan, order and conduct matters
until they are brought into action, and
then each man is to fight as though he
was to gain the battle himself. General
orders are commonly given in time of

General Bouquet—Henry Bouquet's tactics during the Battle of Bushy Run were described by Charles Whittlesey: "The Indians who were assembled at Fort Pitt, left the siege of that place and advanced to meet the force of Boquet, intending to execute a surprise and destroy the whole command. These savages remembered how easily they had entrapped General Braddock, a few years before, by the same movement, and had no doubt of success against Boquet. But he moved always in a hollow square, with his provision train and his cattle in the centre, impressing his men with the idea that a fire might open upon them at any moment. When the important hour arrived, and they were saluted with the discharge of a thousand rifles, accompanied by the .terrific yells of so many savage warriors, arrayed in the livery of demons, the English and provincial troops behaved like veterans, whom nothing could shake. They achieved a complete victory, and drove the allied Indian force beyond the Ohio."

Had no British troops—Colonel Smith may be in error regarding the absence of British troops at Colonel Crawford's defeat in June 1782. A force of Butler's Rangers under Captain William Caldwell was sent from Detroit to assist the Indians when Crawford approached the Sandusky towns from the east.

battle, either to advance or retreat, and is done by a shout or yell, which is well understood, and then they retreat or advance in concert. They are generally well equipped, and exceedingly expert and active in the use of arms. Could it be supposed that undisciplined troops could defeat Generals Braddock, Grant, &c.? It may be said by some that the French were also engaged in this war: true, they were; yet I know it was the Indians that laid the plan, and with small assistance, put it into execution. The Indians had no aid from the French, or any other power, when they besieged Fort Pitt in the year 1763, and cut off the communication for a considerable time, between that post and Fort Loudon, and would have defeated General Bouquet's army, (who were on the way to raise the siege) had it not been for the assistance of the Virginia volunteers. They had no British troops with them when they defeated Colonel Crawford, near the Sandusky, in the time of the American war with Great Britain: or when they defeated Colonel Loughrie, on the Ohio, near the Miami, on his way to meet General Clarke: this was also in the time of the British war. It was the Indians alone that defeated Colonel Todd, in Kentucky, near the Blue licks, in the year 1782; and Colonel Harmer, betwixt the Ohio and Lake Erie, in the year 1790, and General St. Clair, in the year 1791; and it is said that there were more of our men killed at this defeat, than there were in any one battle during our contest with Great Britain. They had no aid

when they fought even the Virginia
rifle-men almost a whole day, at the
Great Kanhawa, in the year 1774; and
when they found they could not prevail
against the Virginians, they made a
most artful retreat. Notwithstanding
they had the Ohio to cross, some
continued firing, whilst others were
crossing the river; in this manner
they proceeded until they all got over,
before the Virginians knew that they had
retreated; and in this retreat they carried
off all their wounded. In the most of the
foregoing defeats, they fought with an
inferior number, though in this, I believe
it was not the case.

Nothing can be more unjustly
represented than the different accounts we
have had of their number from time to
time, both by their own computations,
and that of the British. While I was among
them, I saw the account of the number,
that they in those parts gave to the
French, and kept it by me. When they in
their own council-house, were taking an
account of their number, with a piece of
bark newly stripped, and a small stick,
which answered the end of a slate and
pencil, I took an account of the different
nations and tribes, which I added together,
and found there were not half the number
which they had given the French: and
though they were then their allies, and
lived among them, it was not easy finding
out the deception, as they were a
wandering set, and some of them almost
always in the woods hunting. I asked one
of the chiefs what was their reason for
making such different returns? He said it

At the Battle of Blue
Licks in Kentucky on Au-
gust 19, 1782, there
were four to six hundred
Indians. With them were
Simon Girty, Alexander
McKee, and Captains
William Caldwell and
Matthew Elliott, all
well-known figures in the
British service.

was for political reasons, in order to
obtain greater presents from the French,
by telling them they could not divide such
and such quantities of goods among so
many.

In the year of General Bouquet's last
campaign, 1764, I saw the official return
made by the British officers, of the number
of Indians that were in arms against us
that year, which amounted to thirty
thousand. As I was then a lieutenant in
the British service, I told them I was of
opinion that there was not above one
thousand in arms against us, as they were
divided by Broadstreet's army being then
at Lake Erie. The British officers hooted
at me, and said they could not make
England sensible of the difficulties they
labored under in fighting them, as
England expects that their troops could
fight the undisciplined savages in
America, five to one, as they did the
East-Indians, and therefore my report
would not answer their purpose, as they
could not give an honorable account of
the war, but by augmenting their number.
I am of opinion that from Braddock's war,
until the present time, there never were
more than three thousand Indians, at any
time in arms against us, west of Fort Pitt,
and frequently not half that number.
According to the Indians' own accounts,
during the whole of Braddock's war, or
from 1755, till 1758, they killed or took,
fifty of our people, for one that they lost.
In the war that commenced in the year
1763, they killed, comparatively, few of
our people, and lost more of theirs, as the
frontiers (especially the Virginians) had

learned something of their method of war: yet, they, in this war, according to their own accounts, (which I believe to be true) killed or took ten of our people, for one they lost.

Let us now take a view of the blood and treasure that was spent in opposing comparatively, a few Indian warriors, with only some assistance from the French, the first four years of the war. Additional to the amazing destruction and slaughter that the frontiers sustained, from James River to Susquehanna, and about thirty miles broad; the following campaigns were also carried on against the Indians: —General Braddock's, in the year 1755: Colonel Armstrong's against the Cattanyan town, on the Allegheny, 1757: General Forbes's, in 1758: General Stanwick's, in 1759: General Monkton's, in 1760: Colonel Bouquet's, in 1761— and 1763, when he fought the battle of Brushy Run, and lost above one hundred men, but; by the assistance of the Virginia volunteers, drove the Indians: Colonel Armstrong's, up the West Branch of Susquehanna, in 1763: General Broadstreet's, up Lake Erie, in 1764: General Bouquet's, against the Indians at Muskingum, in 1764: Lord Dunmore's, in 1774: General M'Intosh's, in 1778: Colonel Crawford's, shortly after his, General Clarke's, in 1778—1780: Colonel Bowman's, in 1779: General Clarke's, in 1782—against the Wabash, in 1786: General Logan's against the Shawanees, in 1786: General Wilkinson's, in ----: Colonel Harmer's, in 1790: and General St. Clair's, in 1791; which, in all, are

**Brushy Run**—Bushy Run, twenty-six miles southeast of Fort Pitt, was the site of the previously described battle between Bouquet's column and the Indians in Pontiac's War, on August 5 and 6, 1763. While the Indians were defeated, they inflicted approximately 122 casualties on Bouquet's force. (Military usage of the term casualties always includes those killed, wounded, captured, or missing.)

**Wilkinson**—In May of 1791 Colonel James Wilkinson accompanied General Charles Scott of Kentucky, who led eight hundred mounted Kentuckians in a raid on the Wea villages on the Wabash River. The Indian towns were destroyed and the hostility of the Weas and other northwestern tribes remained unchecked.

twenty-two campaigns, beside smaller expeditions—such as the French Creek expedition, Colonels Edwards's, Loughrie's, &c. All these were exclusive of the number of men that were internally employed as scouting parties, and in erecting forts, guarding stations, &c. When we take the foregoing occurrences into consideration, may we not reasonably conclude, that they are the best disciplined troops in the known world? Is it not the best discipline that has the greatest tendency to annoy the enemy and save their own men? I apprehend that the Indian discipline is as well calculated to answer the purpose in the woods of America, as the British discipline in Flanders: and British discipline, in the woods, is the way to have men slaughtered, with scarcely any chance of defending themselves.

Let us take a view of the benefits we have received, by what little we have learned of their art of war, which cost us dear, and the less we have sustained for want of it, and then see if it will not be well worth our while to retain what we have, and also to endeavor to improve in this necessary branch of business. Though we have made considerable proficiency in this line, and in some respects out-do them, viz. as marksmen, and in cutting our rifles, and keeping them in good order; yet I apprehend, we are far behind in their manoeuvres, or in being able to surprize, or prevent a surprize. May we not conclude that the progress we had made in their art of war, contributed considerably towards our success, in

Cutting our rifles—
Here Smith is writing about one of the skills of a gunsmith known as rifling or cutting a barrel. The inside of a musket barrel is smoothbore, like a shotgun. But the Pennsylvania-Kentucky rifle of the frontiersman had a rifled barrel, that

various respects, when contending with great Britain for liberty? Had the British king attempted to enslave us before Braddock's war, in all probability he might readily have done it, because, except the New-Englanders, who had formerly been engaged in war, with the Indians, we were unacquainted with any kind of war: but after fighting such a subtle and barbarous enemy as the Indians, we were not terrified at the approach of British red-coats.—Was not Burgoyne's defeat accomplished in some measure, by the Indian mode of fighting? and did not Gen. Morgan's rifle-men, and many others, fight with greater success, in consequence of what they had learned of their art of war? Kentucky would not have been settled at the time it was, had the Virginians been altogether ignorant of this method of war.

In Braddock's war, the frontiers were laid waste for above three hundred miles long, and generally about thirty broad, excepting some that were living in forts, and many hundreds, or perhaps thousands, killed or made captives, and horses, and all kinds of property carried off: but, in the next Indian war, though we had the same Indians to cope with, the frontiers almost all stood their ground, because they were by this time, in some measure acquainted with their manoeuvres; and the want of this, in the first war, was the cause of the loss of many hundreds of our citizens, and much treasure.

Though large volumes have been wrote on morality, yet it may be all summed up

is, spiral grooves cut in the bore. An average rifle barrel had seven grooves, with one turn in forty-eight inches. When the rifle was fired, the rifling spun the round lead ball wrapped in a cloth patch, imparting to it greater velocity, range, and accuracy than a smoothbore musket.

If a rifle barrel, after considerable use and wear, lost some of its accuracy, it was "recut" or "freshed out" by a gunsmith, a procedure which deepened the worn rifling and renewed the accuracy of the rifle.

The Indians depended on white gunsmiths for repairs to their firearms, as there were very few Indian gunsmiths. Some Delawares and Wyandots could make gunstocks and do minor repair work. However, the Indians generally requested that traders send black-smiths and gunsmiths to live or stay with them to repair their guns and metal implements.

in saying, do as you would wish to be done by: so the Indians sum up the art of war in the following manner:

The business of the private warriors is to be under command, or punctually to obey orders—to learn to march a-breast in scattered order, so as to be in readiness to surround the enemy, or to prevent being surrounded—to be good marksmen, and active in the use of arms—to practice running—to learn to endure hunger or hardships with patience and fortitude— to tell the truth at all times to their officers, but more especially when sent out to spy the enemy.

<u>Concerning Officers</u>. They say that it would be absurd to appoint a man an officer whose skill and courage had never been tried—that all officers should be advanced only according to merit—that no one man should have the absolute command of an army—that a council of officers are to determine when, and how an attack is to be made—that it is the business of the officers to lay plans to take every advantage of the enemy—to ambush and surprize them, and to prevent being ambushed and surprized themselves— it is the duty of officers to prepare and deliver speeches to the men, in order to annimate and encourage them; and on the march, to prevent the men, at any time, from getting into a huddle, because if the enemy should surround them in this position, they would be exposed to the enemy's fire. It is likewise their business at all times to endeavor to annoy their enemy, and save their own men, and therefore ought never to bring on an

attack without considerable advantage, or
without what appeared to them the sure
prospect of victory, and that with the loss
of few men: and if at any time they should
be mistaken in this, and are like to lose
many men by gaining the victory, it is
their duty to retreat, and wait for a better
opportunity of defeating their enemy,
without the danger of losing so many men.
Their conduct proves that they act upon
these principles, therefore it is, that from
Braddock's war to the present time,
they have seldom ever made an
unsuccessful attack. The battle at the
mouth of the Great Kanhawa, is the
greatest instance of this; and even then,
though the Indians killed about three, for
one they lost, yet they retreated. The loss
of the Virginians in this action, was
seventy killed, and the same number
wounded:—The Indians lost twenty
killed on the field, and eight, who died
afterwards, of their wounds. This was the
greatest loss of men that I ever knew the
Indians to sustain in any one battle. They
will commonly retreat if their men are
falling fast—they will not stand cutting,
like the Highlanders or other British
troops: but this proceeds from a
compliance with their rules of war, rather
than cowardice. If they are surrounded,
they will fight while there is a man of
them alive, rather than surrender. When
Colonel John Armstrong surrounded the
Cattanyan town, on the Allegheny river,
Captain Jacobs, a Delaware chief, with
some warriors, took possession of a house,
defended themselves for some time, and
killed a number of our men. As Jacobs

Battle at the Great
Kanhawa—This battle at
Point Pleasant, Virginia,
where the Kanawha River
flows into the Ohio, was
fought on October 10,
1774, as part of Dun-
more's War. General
Andrew Lewis led an
army of about one
thousand frontier rifle-
men in the battle against
an equal number of
Shawnee led by Corn-
stalk. The Indians at-
tacked the frontiersmen
who used Indian battle
tactics against them.
After an all day battle, the
Shawnee were forced to
withdraw across the Ohio.
   Taken with General
Bouquet's Battle of Bushy
Run in 1763, this battle
at the Kanawha fulfills
Smith's June 1756 predic-
tion that the settlers
would not only learn the
Indians' mode of war but
"turn it upon them."

could speak English, our people called on him to surrender: he said that he and his men were warriors, and they would all fight while life remained. He was again told that they should be well used, if they would only surrender; and if not, the house should be burned down over their heads:—Jacobs replied he could eat fire: and when the house was in a flame, he, and they that were with him, came out in a fighting position, and were all killed. As they are a sharp, active kind of people, and war is their principal study, in this they have arrived at considerable perfection. We may learn of the Indians what is useful and laudable, and at the same time lay aside their barbarous proceedings. It is much to be lamented that some of our frontier riflemen are too prone to imitate them in their inhumanity. During the British war, a considerable number of men from below Fort Pitt, crossed the Ohio, and marched into a town of Friendly Indians, chiefly Delawares, who professed the Moravian religion. As the Indians apprehended no danger, they neither lifted arms nor fled. After these rifle-men were sometime in the town, and the Indians altogether in their power, in cool blood, they massacred the whole town, without distinction of age or sex. This was an act of barbarity beyond any thing I ever knew to be committed by the savages themselves.

Why have we not made greater proficiency in the Indian art of war? Is it because we are too proud to imitate them, even though it should be a means of preserving the lives of many of our

Massacre—Refers to the March 1782 destruction of over ninety Christian Indians and their village, Gnadenhutten. This village settlement was founded in 1772 by David Zeisberger and John Heckewelder. In his description of the Indian children Heckewelder underlines the brutality of frontiersmen avenging recent Indian attacks:

citizens? No! We are not above borrowing language from them, such as homony, pone, tomahawk, &c. which is of little or no use to us. I apprehend that the reasons why we have not improved more in this respect, are as follows: no important acquisition is to be obtained but by attention and diligence; and as it is easier to learn to move and act in concert, in close order, in the open plain, than to act in concert in scattered order, in the woods; so it is easier to learn our discipline, than the Indian manoeuvres. They train up their boys to the art of war from the time they are twelve or fourteen years of age; whereas the principal chance our people had of learning, was by observing their movements when in action against us. I have been long astonished that no one has wrote upon this important subject, as their art of war would not only be of use to us in case of another rupture with them; but were only part of our men taught this art, accompanied with our continental discipline, I think no European power, after trial, would venture to shew its head in the American woods.

If what I have wrote should meet the approbation of my countrymen, perhaps I may publish more upon this subject, in a future edition.

"Their tender years, innocent countenances and tears made no impression on these pretended white Christians. These children were all butchered with the rest."

It was mainly in rage and revenge for the Gnadenhutten massacre that the Delawares burnt Colonel Crawford at the stake a few months later, even though he was not involved in the massacre.

A Pennsylvania militia officer named Williamson was in command of the raiders at Gnadenhutten. He was also one of the officers with Crawford's force but escaped capture during the defeat and rout of unfortunate Colonel Crawford.

## END.

# Bibliography*

Adney, Edwin Tappan and Howard I. Chapelle. *The Bark Canoes and Skin Boats of North America.* Washington: Smithsonian Institution, 1964.
*American Indian Art Form and Tradition.* Walker Art Center and the Minneapolis Institute of Arts. New York: E. P. Dutton & Co., Inc., 1972.

Bakeless, John. *Master of the Wilderness, Daniel Boone.* New York: William Morrow & Company, 1942.
Banta, R. E. *The Ohio.* New York: Rinehart & Company, 1949.
Bond, Beverley W., Jr. *The Foundations of Ohio, The History of the State of Ohio,* Vol. 1. Columbus: Ohio Historical Society, 1941.
Boyd, Thomas. *Simon Girty, The White Savage.* New York: Minton, Balch & Company, 1928.
Brickell, John. "Narrative of John Brickell's Captivity Among the Delaware Indians," *The American Pioneer* I (1842): 43-59.
Brown, Orley E., ed. *The Captivity of Jonathan Alder and His Life With the Indians.* Alliance, Ohio: O. E. Brown, 1965.
Buchman, Randall L. *The Historic Indian in Ohio.* Columbus: Ohio Historical Society, 1976.
Butterfield, C. W. *An Historical Account of the Expedition Against Sandusky Under Colonel William Crawford in 1782.* Cincinnati: R. Clarke & Co., 1873.
———. *History of the Girtys.* Cincinnati: R. Clarke & Co., 1890.

Carter, W. H. *North American Indian Trade Silver.* 2 vols. London, Ontario: Engel Printing, 1971.
Catlin, George. *Letters and Notes About North American Indians.* New York: C. N. Potter, 1975.
Cline, Walter M. *The Muzzle Loading Rifle Then and Now.* Huntington, W.V.: The Standard Press, 1942.
Culin, Stewart. *Games of the North American Indians.* Bureau of American Ethnology, 24th Annual Report (1902-1903). Washington: U.S. Government Printing Office, 1904.

---

* Background and source materials compiled by John J. Barsotti.

Darlington, William M. *Christopher Gist's Journals, With Historical, Geographical and Ethnological Notes and Biographies of His Contemporaries.* Pittsburgh: J. R. Weldin and Co., 1893.

Dillin, John G. W. *The Kentucky Rifle.* York, Pa.: Trimmer Printing, Inc., 1959.

Doddridge, Joseph. *Notes on the Settlement and Indian Wars of The Western Parts of Virginia and Pennsylvania.* Pittsburgh: John S. Ritenour and William T. Lindsey, 1912.

Edmonds, Walter D. *In the Hands of the Senecas.* Boston: Little, Brown & Company, 1947.

———. *The Musket and the Cross.* Boston: Little, Brown & Company, 1968.

Foreman, Grant. *The Last Trek of the Indians.* Chicago: University of Chicago Press, 1946.

Galloway, William. *Old Chillicothe.* Xenia, Ohio: The Buckeye Press, 1934.

Hamilton, T. M. *Native American Bows.* York, Pa.: George Shumway Publishers, 1972.

Hanna, Charles A. *The Wilderness Trail, or the Ventures and Adventures of the Pennsylvania Traders on the Allegheny Path.* 2 vols. New York: G. P. Putnam's Sons, 1911.

Hanson, Charles E. *The Northwest Gun.* Lincoln: Nebraska State Historical Society, 1955.

Heard, J. Norman. *White into Red, A Study of the Assimilation of White Persons Captured by Indians.* Metucken, N.J.: The Scarecrow Press, Inc., 1973.

Henry, Alexander. *Travels and Adventures in Canada and the Indian Territories Between the Years 1760 and 1776.* Toronto: G. N. Morang, 1901.

Hodge, F. W., ed. *Handbook of American Indians North of Mexico.* 2 vols. Bureau of American Ethnology, Bulletin 30. Washington: U.S. Government Printing Office, 1907.

Howe, Henry. *Historical Collections of Ohio.* Cincinnati: Derby, Bradley & Co., 1847.

Hulbert, A. B. and William N. Schwarze, eds. "David Zeisberger's History of the North American Indians." *The Ohio Archaeological and Historical Society Publications* 19 (1910): 1-189.

———. *The Ohio River, A Course of Empire.* New York: G. P. Putnam's Sons, 1906.

Jillson, Willard Rouse. *A Bibliography of the Life and Writings of Col. James Smith. . . .* Frankfort: Kentucky Historical Society, 1947.

———. *Rare Kentucky Books.* Louisville: The Standard Printing Company, 1939.

Kauffman, Henry J. *The Pennsylvania-Kentucky Rifle.* Harrisburg, Pa.: Stackpole Co., 1960.

Kenton, Edna, ed. *The Indians of North America.* 2 vols. New York: Harcourt, Brace & Company, 1927.
——. *Simon Kenton His Life and Period, 1755-1836.* Garden City, N.Y.: Doubleday, Doran & Company, Inc., 1930.
Kuck, Robert. *Tomahawks Illustrated.* Xenia, Ohio: Aldine Printing Co., 1977.

Leland, Charles G. *Algonquin Legends of New England.* Detroit: Singing Tree Press, 1968.
——. "Legends of the Passamaquoddy." *The Century Magazine XXVIII* (Sept. 1884): 668-677.
"Life and Travels of Col. James Smith." *National Magazine of American History* 1 (1920): 228-245.

McClure, David. *Diary of David McClure, Doctor of Divinity, 1748-1820.* New York: The Knickerbocker Press, 1899.
Miles, Charles. *Indian and Eskimo Artifacts of North America.* New York: The Henry Regnery Co., 1963.
Morgan, Fred. "Wild Rice Harvest," *The Beaver, Magazine of the North.* Autumn, 1960, p. 24.
Orchard, W. C. *Beads and Beadwork of the American Indians.* New York: Museum of the American Indian, 1929.

Parkman, Francis. *Conspiracy of Pontiac and the Indian War After the Conquest of Canada.* New York: A. L. Burt, 1902.
——. *Francis Parkman's Works.* Boston: Little, Brown & Company Publishers, 1902.
——. *The Struggle for a Continent.* Boston: Little, Brown & Company, 1902.
Patterson, William D. *Beginnings of the American Rectangular Land Survey System 1784-1800.* Chicago: University of Chicago Press, 1957.
Peckham, Howard H. *Pontiac and the Indian Uprising.* Princeton: Princeton University Press, 1947.
Petersen, Eugene T. *Gentlemen on the Frontier: A Pictorial Record of the Culture of Michilimackinac.* Mackinac Island, Mich.: Mackinac Island State Park Commission, 1964.
Peterson, Harold L. *American Indian Tomahawks.* New York: Museum of the American Indian, 1965.

Richter, Conrad. *A Country of Strangers.* New York: A. A. Knopf, 1966.
——. *The Light in the Forest.* New York: A. A. Knopf, 1966.
Rush, Benjamin. *Medical Inquiries and Observations,* Vol. 4. Philadelphia: Thomas Dobson, 1796.
Russell, Carl P. *Firearms, Traps and Tools of the Mountain Men.* New York: A. A. Knopf, 1967.

"Saga of James Smith." *American History Illustrated* 5 (1970): June p. 34; August p. 36; October p. 34.
Sandoz, Mari. *The Beaver Men, Spearheads of Empire.* New York: Hastings House Publishers, 1964.

Schaff, Morris. *Etna and Kirkersville*. Boston: Houghton, Mifflin and Company, 1905.

Seaver, James E. *A Narrative of the Life of Mrs. Mary Jemison*. New York: Random House, 1929.

Simpson, Joseph. *The Story of Buckeye Lake*. Columbus, Ohio: The Hann & Adair Printing Company, 1912.

Smith, James. *An Account of the Remarkable Occurrences . . .* Cincinnati: Robert Clarke & Co., 1870.

———. *An Account of the Remarkable Occurrences . . .* Philadelphia: Grigg & Elliot, 1834.

———. *An Account of the Remarkable Occurrences . . .* Lexington: John Bradford, 1799.

Spencer, Oliver M. *Indian Captivity*. Ann Arbor: University Microfilms, Inc., 1966.

Tucker, Glenn. *Tecumseh, Vision of Glory*. Indianapolis: Bobbs-Merrill, 1956.

Vanderwerth, W. C. *Indian Oratory. Famous Speeches by Noted Indian Chieftains*. New York: Ballantine Books, Inc., 1972.

Van Every, Dale. *Ark of Empire; The American Frontier, 1784-1803*. New York: William Morrow & Company, 1963.

———. *A Company of Heroes; The American Frontier, 1775-1783*. New York: William Morrow & Company, 1962.

———. *Disinherited: The Lost Birthright of the American Indian*. New York: William Morrow & Company, 1966.

———. *The Final Challenge; The American Frontier, 1804-1845*. New York: William Morrow & Company, 1964.

———. *Forth to the Wilderness; The First American Frontier, 1754-1774*. New York: William Morrow & Company, 1961.

———. *Men of the Western Waters; A Second Look at the First Americans*. Boston: Houghton, Mifflin and Company, 1956.

Wallace, Paul A. W. *Indians in Pennsylvania*. Harrisburg: The Pennsylvania Historical and Museum Commission, 1964.

Weslager, C. A. *The Delaware Indians, A History*. New Brunswick, N.J.: Rutgers University Press, 1972.

Wilcox, Frank. *Ohio Indian Trials*. Cleveland: The Gates Press, 1933.

Withers, Alexander Scott. *Chronicles of Border Warfare*. Cincinnati: Robert Clarke Company, 1908.

Woodward, Arthur. *Denominators of the Fur Trade*. Pasadena: Socio-Technical Publications, 1970.